Where To, Black Man?

BY ED SMITH

Quadrangle Books

Chicago 1967

TO ESTHER, PEGGY, AND JOAN
    for their generosity

DR. MARY L. SEQUEL
    for her friendship

WARREN AND LOUISE
    for their tolerance

KWAME NKRUMAH
    for the mistakes he didn't make

AFRICA AND THE PEACE CORPS
    for the ideals of their endeavors

THE STUDENT NONVIOLENT
COORDINATING COMMITTEE
    for its militant honesty and courage

THE WORLD'S PEOPLE OF COLOR
    for our common struggle
    to destroy oppression

PREFACE

The political and social face of Africa shifts so inexorably
that even the most earnest and scholarly attempt to pin
down its essence is necessarily outdated before the ink
has dried on the printer's type. This diary spans about
eighteen months of some two years I served as a Peace
Corps Volunteer in the Republic of Ghana. In the short
space of time between the termination of my tour and
the publication of these experiences, several African nations have been radically shaken by military revolts and
shifts in leadership. Nigeria, once America's bonus baby
in West Africa, seems irrevocably torn by tribal and
regional dissension. Kwame Nkrumah has been summarily
deposed as President of Ghana by a "loyal" army, and has
accepted an embarrassing exile in the Republic of Guinea.

Nonetheless, since the hindsight view of history is
usually the most amusing, my diary may provide bedtime
reading for the weary of heart and the hawkers of concern
for a continent that is destined to command more and
more influence in the affairs of our increasingly frag-
mented world polity. The diary has been described as a
"brutally honest account of how one man saw himself and
the Peace Corps and Ghana during a particular, limited
period. It is a record of neither high international diplo-

macy or a simple, happy life among the delightful, fascinating Ghanaians. It is a record of Ed Smith in a world community where no one can go home again."

I had many sources of encouragement and inspiration during the writing and preparation for publication of the diary. Dr. David Apter, professor of political science and Director of the Institute of International Studies at the University of California, Berkeley, was solely responsible for convincing me that keeping a Peace Corps diary could be a worthwhile venture. Without his constant encouragement there would certainly be no *Where To, Black Man?* Professor St. Clair Drake of Roosevelt University, a long-time Africanist and personal friend of not a few Sub-Saharan African leaders, is the most inspiring human being with whom I have had the pleasure to share a few beers, and he helped me greatly.

To be sure, there are others. Without Mrs. Irish Kapil's friendship and instigation, the diary would be still collecting dust in some half-forgotten recess of my collection of African artifacts. Typing a manuscript is a task of gigantic proportions, and I express deepest gratitude to Libby Jenkins who worked long unpaid hours on the early drafts. Her husband, Dr. George Jenkins, helped in the early editing. Sue Philipson, my editor, provided welcome assistance on the final draft. The original handwritten diary is about three times as long as this book, and without her perseverance the reader would be condemned to details of big and little mosquitoes, moonlit and moonless nights, and lonely bush excursions. Thanks is also due to Ivan Dee, Quadrangle's managing editor; a more considerate, though a no-nonsense, friend a first book writer never had. Others who contributed indirectly in the making of this book include Barbara Boseker, Kathy Ullrich, Jerry and Mary Parson, Dr. R. Wray Strowig, Mr. and Mrs. Daryl Rasmussen, Joan Hugl, Esther White, Dean and

8

Mrs. Frank Himmelman, Carol Bodey, Lilly Gates, Vida Kumi, my friends and students in Ghana, activist friends in Alabama and Wisconsin, and many returned Peace Corps Volunteers.

To these and to those other never-named souls who always read and make critical comments on manuscripts, I am eternally indebted. The reader can rest assured, however, that what appears in the book is an actual account of my life, the easy and hard times, in Ghana. There is no juggling; only names have been changed to protect the innocent. For my friends, enemies, and neutrals who nevertheless feel identified in the diary, I hasten to add that no embarrassment or ridicule is intended and hope that any such implications are excused in the interest of truth and authenticity.

ED SMITH

Milwaukee, Wisconsin
June 1967

9

From Alabama to

the Peace Corps

On the day John F. Kennedy officially inaugurated the Peace Corps in 1961, thousands of Americans found a very personal answer to a very personal request: "Ask not what your country can do for you, but what you can do for your country." For me it meant a determination to puncture the web of racism that kept prisoner all people of color everywhere.

It seemed incredible that a Negro would want to sacrifice two more years of a life that had been molded out of nothing *but* sacrifice. But from Birmingham, Alabama, to De Kalb, Illinois, I had come to know and despise the glaring hypocrisy of a society that loudly proclaimed its liberal ethic to the world, yet deliberately held millions of its own citizens in bondage. What W. E. B. DuBois termed "living behind the Veil" was a horrible reality for black people: for us—two cousins and me—it meant living in a three-room battered-frame house with our maternal grandmother (our parents were separated). As boys we really had to hustle. Many were the frosty mornings when, age six, we were roused from bed by a brutal but well-meaning uncle who lived nearby and ordered us to chop wood for the stove, start a fire, feed the chickens, or scramble off to the white neighborhoods to fill tin buckets with food

or clothing from their garbage pails. And after filling our buckets we would journey through the streets and stuff our pockets with cigarette butts, which would be unwrapped and rewrapped in newspaper or cigarette rollers. These long butts were hard to come by where we lived, because our one paved street offered only strands of scattered tobacco, all that was left from *our* neighbors' weeds.

What we couldn't eat from our salvage, we fed to the chickens or gave to the neighbors for their hogs in return for some of the meat during killing season; what we couldn't wear, we cut up for patches—to be used over worn-out patches. Our only other means of support was an occasional check from my cousins' father (my own father had abandoned my mother), our grandmother's monthly welfare check—$8—and the generosity of a sympathetic uncle in Chicago.

In those days there was much shame but little guilt, for everybody but the preacher's son and those whose fathers were successful gamblers or whisky dealers was in the same boat. Garbage collecting was a lesson in free-enterprise competition, and nobody stopped to consider the infection or disease that might be won along with the booty. It was always heartwarming to enter a really productive alley at the break of dawn and find the cans undisturbed; it was always frantic when others were several cans up on us. Rare were the days when we returned home with empty buckets, and our grandmother was always more than delighted to take on the delicate job of deciding which items were to go where. Kotex, discarded prophylactics, and other household "appliances" never prevented us from digging deeper into the cans; such items were simply objects of laughter, or, in some cases, scorn.

After school and on weekends, we would compete for whose lawnmower (itself usually a product of a fruitful al-

ley foray) got to trim the already manicured lawns of the "white folk." Digging in a nearby creek bed (I shudder to think that we sometimes swam in those polluted, snake-infested pools) for worms to sell to white fishermen was another popular means of earning spending money. (Negro fishermen dug their own.) As soon as we reached adolescence, some of us were promoted to biking drugs for the local pharmacy, scrubbing windows and floors, and carrying chunks of ice for local Negroes who could not yet afford refrigerators. Young and old relished the sale of a fought-over baseball bagged as a foul or homer from the many Black and White Baron (segregated teams in those days) baseball games, which we had sneaked into by scaling twelve- or fifteen-foot fences. Many a kid left part of a finger impaled on the top in his rush to escape club-wielding protectors of the peace. (The cops always seemed to wait in the shadows of the stands until we had just reached the point of no return on the fence.)

Like the Malcolm X's, Richard Wrights, and Claude Browns before us, some of us peddled moonshine for the community big hats. It was about this time, during my early teens, that I found myself with a terrific yen to travel, see faces other than the tormented ones around me; so, one sunny spring morning, with no more than fifty cents in my pocket, I hit out for the "yellow brick road"—only it was a beat-up highway—and after hiking seventeen miles, found the Wizard of Oz—only it was an old, bent lady collecting coal, who, sensing my desperation, sent me off to the local bootlegger's house, where I was to spend one year of pure hell. The belt-buckle beatings meted out by my uncle were as nothing to the almost absolute rejection and isolation a childless bootlegger and his wife managed to provide. I hitchhiked back to Birmingham.

It was there, at the age of seventeen, that I, like the

African of the bush living far from the head of the colonial octopus, found life too immediate in its demands and too piercing in its rebuke to bother about what was *making* it that way. Let the old folks rant and rave about the wickedness of Mr. Charlie behind the safety of closed doors, vowing to "get theirs back" when the time came. I was too busy fighting for air. Only once did I catch a hint of something macabre at work. It was a Saturday morning, and I had gone to a white family's home to earn the one or two bucks for a day of scrubbing and mowing. At lunch time the wife gave me permission to eat in the kitchen while they ate in the dining room, but the incensed husband so strenuously objected that I was forced to retreat to the backyard among his fine breed of hunting dogs. To this day I remember the swarms of flies that visited my plate, the rank odor of pee in my nostrils, and the nausea that came not from these things but from allowing myself to be one of Charlie's dogs—even for a little while.

When my grandmother died in 1954, our "neighbor" uncle saw no reason why he shouldn't move his own family into the rent-free house, so we were forced to hit the road. Our chances seemed better if we split up, so my cousins went their way, and I went mine: dropped out of school and joined the Air Force. But it didn't take me long to learn that Negroes had their problems in the service, too. In fact, I thought it was worse for the Negro soldier in some ways. Race relations were anything but smooth when a white G.I. could be buddy-buddy with a Negro on base and yet cross the street to avoid him when on pass. On Guam, in England, and in Saigon, Negroes and whites retired to separate off-base clubs, and, in the case of Japan, whole towns were reserved for "whites only." A black American who visited certain towns after dark risked life and limb in the true Mississippi fashion. According to some old hands who had been there, when Negro Ameri-

cans arrived on Guam following President Truman's desegregation order, it was not at all uncommon to see a dark-skinned Micronesian staring expectantly at a dark-skinned Negro G.I.'s posterior, hoping to see a long hairy tail protruding. (The white G.I.'s had told them that "Negroes are monkeys and live in trees.")

The rejection I experienced in that most segregated of large U.S. cities, Chicago, and later in provincial De Kalb, Illinois, was hardly worse than what I had been forced to accept even in uniform. So for me, a trip to Ghana had to be something other than what I'm sure it was for white volunteers. I would be serving, not just in another underdeveloped country, but in an independent country of black people striving to demonstrate to the world their ability to conduct their own affairs and determine their own future.

Originally assigned to teach in Nigeria, I was quite disappointed when Washington asked me to teach in Ghana instead. Our press had done a convincing job of painting Nigeria as the budding "new democracy in black Africa" and an even better one of proving Ghana at best a socialist dictatorship and at worst a repressive communist puppet state. But a few weeks later I had forgotten that I had ever preferred Nigeria. One country was the same as another in that great mother country—Black Africa!

What then, could a white volunteer know of my pain when our chartered plane landed at Accra airport and I saw that cluster of World War II vintage buildings in various stages of disrepair, with a terminal whose interior decor gave the appearance of a tired and antiquated Haitian frontier post? What could he know of my bitterness and disillusionment when I watched Ghanaian transport drivers stopping their already overladen lorries on the highway and begging the forgiveness of a white volunteer because the lorry had no room for him? Or of my hostility

19

when I heard Ghanaian girls begging white male volunteers to give them "white babies"?

But neither could the white PCV know of my elation upon seeing blacks in every walk of life and doing every kind of job—cabinet ministers, businessmen, city planners, university teachers, police chiefs . . . Or of my admiration for an academic curriculum that was every bit as demanding as its equivalent back home.

Nor could the white PCV understand the Negro American's easy tolerance of admittedly unprofitable "prestige projects," such as Black Star Square, a purely nonfunctional and extremely costly landmark. But then, why should he? This was not his ancestral land which had achieved political freedom after better than four hundred years of colonial domination and exploitation; which, with an 80 per cent illiteracy rate in 1951, had by 1964 a compulsory primary and secondary educational system, plus three institutions of higher learning with a student body numbering in the thousands and one of the best student-faculty ratios in the world. Nor was this his leader—a man of color—"standing up and telling it like it is" to Mr. Charlie. New modern highways, small and large industries in villages and cities, hospitals, and higher per capita incomes were all signs of a free and progressive Ghana that could only warm and win the hearts of an oppressed group of lost brothers and sisters who had far less to be proud about.

Thus it was with the highest expectations that I took on my first official assignment in Ghana—teaching high school in Half Assini, a rural village of perhaps two thousand inhabitants, separated from the Ivory Coast only by a large lagoon and nestled deep in a tropical rain forest. Survival during the long rainy season, when overland transportation was severely curtailed along the only road into the area, was always a risky business, since the town

20

was rich only in coconuts and depended on other areas of the country for sustenance.

The name "Half Assini" is said to be derived from the division of one village, now known as Big Assini, but having a population of less than five hundred. Scattered around Half Assini in the deep recesses of the forest and on the lagoon itself are numerous other Nzima villages that have even less access to the goods and services of the outside world, and it is said that many of these villagers have never seen a foreigner—white *or* black. Schools here (where there are any) are still of the bush variety—constructions of forest bamboo, a thick clay, and palm leaves, with dirt floors.

Despite being situated on the edge of the Atlantic, Nzimas do not take to the water. They are the only southern group who have historically refused to bolster their diet with the readily available fish, preferring to depend on food from the undependable trucks from the east. Only the lagoon dwellers—and they apparently out of sheer necessity—could be described as a fishing people.

Axim, the nearest town of any size to Half Assini, with about five thousand people, lies sixty miles to the east. Here live the bulk of the Ahanta, close relatives of the Nzima. Both groups speak the most difficult of Ghana's fifty dialects, and the only ones that remain unintelligible to other Twi-speaking Ghanaians. The government is presently expanding the clinic here (until recently the only medical facility serving far southwestern Ghana) into a full hospital with modern equipment and a competently trained staff, but until it is complete, one still has to go to Takoradi, a city ninety miles east of Axim, for modern medical treatment. There is also a small clinic in a tiny village some thirteen miles east of Half Assini, its staff consisting only of a superintendent and a midwife, but only in dire emergency would one go there.

21

Except for one all-purpose store, Nzimaland was practically ignored by British colonialists. They instituted no medical service, and schools remained a monopoly of various missionary societies. Indeed, until the Gold Coast became independent Ghana, not one high school lay between Half Assini and Takoradi, an area said to contain an estimated quarter of Ghana's seven million-plus population. The Nzima proudly claimed that they had "successfully resisted British colonization efforts," but the truth of the matter was that there was little worth conquering, so the Queen had simply left matters in the hands of local chiefs.

It was into such a setting that Ole Bos and I found ourselves catapulted after eight weeks of concentrated preparation at Berkeley, California, and one week of "orientation" in Accra at the University of Ghana. Ole Bos and I: one the middle-class son of a college professor, the other a "deprived" ward of even more deprived relatives; one politically conservative by training and commitment, the other bound by the cruel circumstances of life to an irrevocable fight to the death for radical political and social change; one a disinterested participant in a grand ideal of paternal service to a backward people, the other chained to an active program of aggressively asserting his and his people's right to be; one white, the other black—Ole Bos and me, both American city boys going to the country.

What Ole Bos's expectations were, what he hoped to give or gain, remain a mystery to me: we were never on the same wavelength. As for me, this was a place where I might *reach* someone with my people's tragic experiences in Mr. Charlie's America. But I was to be disappointed: too many years of "indirect rule" had cheated the African of an awareness of a Machiavellian scheme that was still at work wherever the black man allowed his white oppressor to reign victorious. He could talk about the unification

22

of Africa but not about a unity of black men throughout the world.

Half Assini Secondary School was typical of a score of new high schools constructed under the Convention People's party government's Accelerated Development Plan: several brightly painted basic buildings, including blocks for administration, science, arts and crafts, classrooms, and dormitories. The hope was eventually to make each compound or campus a small, more or less self-sustaining independent community in which teachers as well as students would be required to live. After two years Half Assini already had three single-family staff bungalows, a larger home for the headmaster (principal), and a three-story, six-flat apartment building for junior masters (teachers), where Ole Bos and I had adjoining five-room apartments on the top floor. We also had access to two detached rear rooms, traditionally reserved for visiting relatives, but for us, quarters for our houseboys.

The compound proper covered perhaps five acres, donated to the government by a wealthy old gentleman who was the "town philanthropist" and "uncrowned king."

The teaching staff—excluding us there were ten Ghanaians, six of whom were Fantis—served a student body of approximately two hundred first-, second-, and third-year pupils. Only the principal (a Fanti) and Ackah (an Nzima), later to become principal himself, were college graduates; the educational background of the other masters ranged anywhere from eight to twelve years. In general, the Nzimas were academically less qualified than the Fantis, who have long been considered Ghana's most urbane and educated group—a fact that hardly guaranteed friendly inter-tribal relations. Having been isolated both politically and culturally since time immemorial, it was natural for the Nzimas to distrust and even refuse to patronize a school dominated by representatives of a more fortunate people.

23

Indeed, many area parents refused to send their children to the school, and the principal, in his own words, "had to beat the bush and make long hazardous treks to plead for students."

Fantis also dominated the town's important civil service positions, thus forming with the teachers a kind of alien and outcast elite. It was toward this group that I naturally gravitated: they were sophisticated, spoke English well, were up on current events, and, more than the Nzima ever did, showed an awareness of our common history. It was just this identification, however, that left me stranded and alone when virtually all the Fantis transferred or resigned a few months after our arrival. The school's Board of Governors was determined to install one of their own Nzima tribesmen as principal, though the chap was clearly not qualified. (Come to think of it, my own qualifications don't sound so great when I remember how I spent long afternoons during those desperately lonely months throwing balloons and shillings to the kids below from my veranda. But they were as needy as I was lonely . . .)

I wouldn't even have the slight consolation of keeping my diary these first five months: I had been told on arrival that Peace Corps law forbids volunteers from entering the arena of local politics, and particularly from commenting on political issues if they should be involuntarily involved. There were always "those on the prowl for evidence of the Peace Corps' commitment to a subversive ideology," and a diary was all they needed to confirm their distrust. People don't take well to secrets unless they're in on them.

Thus I include one entry here—the first of many to fill several notebooks during my stay in Ghana—rather than at the beginning of my diary, since it is the only one I wrote

24

down in all those early months, so intimidated was I by all those "guardians of the peace."

JANUARY 10

Throughout Ghana, towns and villages were alive with people dancing in the streets; courtly, dignified processions of elders, their heads held high; children skipping after, waving scarves all colors of the rainbow to the blare of trumpet, the rumble of drum. The air reverberated with song, a people's tribute to their Leader and Liberator. But here in Half Assini only the drowsy hum of insect wings could be heard in the streets; all was quiet, heavy, close . . . No celebration at all—in the Liberator's own home town—but then, equally puzzling, there was no Convention People's party office here to organize such affairs. What did it matter if the locals were right, that no displays were necessary here of all places, since everyone knew the citizenry were fanatically loyal to Nkrumah and the party? Surely there could be no harm in showing it . . . Unless I had failed to detect something more immediate beneath the seemingly unruffled surface of this modest little bush town—something that concerned many Ghanaians, not just those here, and, as I would learn all too soon . . . me.

HALF ASSINI

MARCH 3

While at a friend's home today, I chanced to meet a South African couple who had fled their homeland: he, a white, had dared to marry a "colored" woman. Their most fervent desire was to return to a new South Africa where they could rear their young son in a relatively secure environment. That they were sincere in this desire was beyond doubt. Like many a fearful expatriate, however, these exiles said one thing and thought quite another: "loyalty to President Nkrumah's interpretation of socialism" was all too often a veil behind which lurked a virulent antisocialism.

There was another who wished to return—but to her post in Togo. A menstrual cycle gone wild had sent her fleeing to the Corps' doctor in Accra. She passed through Half Assini on her way . . .

MARCH 4

The confusion over "American vs. English" teaching methods reared its ugly head again. My students think that all teachers, whether they like it or not, are obliged to pay strict attention to the Ministry of Education syllabus, which happens to be English and from which all questions on their final exams will be drawn. I assured them

29

that they needn't panic at the slightest deviation from that worthy program!

Later in the day the principal of the local government elementary school came by to check on the rumor that I was asking friends at home to send books for the nonexistent school library. Learning it was true, he literally went down on all fours and begged me to plead his school's cause to my friends. He left pleased that he would share in the bounty.

MARCH 5

Another of those AM to PM with nothing-in-between days. Jeep was on the bum again, but I didn't care if the damned hood fell off: I had to get away from this place, even for a couple of hours. On the way to town, I stopped off at Esiama, a small coastal village that had been a thriving commercial center in the days when men went up country to work the gold fields. The gold had long since run out, the palatial homes reduced to shambling ruins, and what had once been considered a booming economy could now be measured in terms of a small outdoor market where housewives bought day-to-day foodstuffs. A tiny, isolated little world, so unlike the one "outside," glistening with spanking new hotels, all shiny and bright. And if they weren't so bright inside—bathrooms that looked like outhouses moved in, rooms as small as prison cells—this was, after all, an age of transition for Ghana. A good thing to remember on this of all days: Independence Day.

On my way back I would hear Nkrumah's broadcast to the nation, the one and only form of celebration this year: too many patriotic Ghanaians had been killed by traitors. I would measure the rise and fall of that powerful voice, like the beat of vigorous young hearts, and hear my own heart responding in a surge of emotion said to be reserved only

for one's homeland. "Today there is a new government
. . . Ghana's independence means to other African countries the total liberation of the African continent . . ." The
day would come when all of those nations would know
Ghana's achievements for their own: new airways, shipping lines, military academies; African currency, civil
service, national research councils . . . Life would be good
because it would be their own.

From what I had already observed, however, independence meant different things to different people, and not
always good. To my students, most of whom were still in
elementary school at the time, it meant the day "when
British rule was abolished," "when the imperialists were
kicked out"; in other words, when they were at last free
from, not free *to*: realization of their individual and collective potential was not nearly as strong a concept as
"freedom from the Crown."

But to others—people from all walks of life—and there
were many, independence was still to be won: "freedom
from the Crown," "freedom from the present regime"—
for these people the terms had become interchangeable.
They even accused Nkrumah's government of perpetuat-
ing the same injustices that had prevailed under Crown administration: keeping the people ignorant, restricting their
freedom of speech and action, taking advantage of their
labor and giving little in return . . . True, they had will-
ingly given their support prior to Ghana's independence,
but Nkrumah and his party had betrayed the revolution . . .

So, then, here was Ghana, vigorously struggling to bring
to the surface Africa's glorious past that it might become
her present, reaching out for the loyalty of her people, only
to be met with distrust, fear, indifference. Nor was this
terribly surprising when one considers the fact that these
people had *colonial,* not *African,* history jammed down
their throats for a helluva long time, so that a bus driver

could even today, with stern conviction, state flatly that "Africans are black because the sun is hotter in Africa." (He had fought in Burma and India for the British, helping them save the world for democracy. *Whose* democracy? I couldn't ask even my students: they were still cutting their teeth on *The World Before Britain,* trying to understand a text obviously directed toward a very different culture from their own. "In our Bible . . ." "We all know the Bible story of . . ." Well, gentlemen, not all students are Christians, and not all know the Bible story of . . .)

But at least Ghana, unlike most of the other independent countries, considers its people's history significant enough to warrant an Institute of African Culture, an Institute of African Study at the university, and a Bureau of Ghana Languages. And it won't be long before schools like mine reflect that burgeoning thing called African Personality.

MARCH 8

Several of my students came by this morning to say that classes had been canceled for the day: children from all parts of the country would be taking entrance exams for high school. It has become disturbingly characteristic of the principal to forget to let his teachers in on such matters.

So, having nothing to do, I decided to go to the library: if Ghana was truly in left field politically, as America would believe, surely her school libraries would be repositories of socialist and communist literature. Brushing aside the Western books (a legacy of colonialism), I turned my attention to the subscribed periodicals, and discovered that, of a total of seventy-five, approximately ten were from Eastern countries and the People's Republic of China, and of those, only the *World Marxist Review* could

be considered hard-core propagandist literature. Surprisingly, West Germany led the field for the West.

From a quick look through the library cards, it was clear that very few students read even those Eastern publications that dealt with cultural rather than revolutionary material. Anyway, at least Ghana's schools were receiving a liberal sampling of socialist literature.

On my way back, I saw that the sign over the gate of the poultry farm had been removed. This had been a pet project of mine, begun with the help of the students in the months that preceded this diary. We had named it after the school's first principal, one of our principal's bitterest enemies, and were still suffering the consequences. Many long, hard, hot hours had been spent building fences, clearing the jungle growth, begging funds and using my own, sneaking the Peace Corps' jeep to drive fifty or sixty miles to purchase wire or hens, only to have nearly everything stolen by a bunch of disgruntled teachers. I had not only been accused of undermining the authority of the new principal, but also reprimanded for managing something that was by right only a Ghanaian's property. Well, now they could take their damn poultry farm! This was their school, their country. They could take it and shove it!

But when I got home, my anger had already been replaced by a deep-down sadness. I paced the room restlessly, tried to read, couldn't, tried to believe that it was better to be anything else but an outsider, couldn't . . . What about the story my cop friend Armah had told me about a local market woman who had been apprehended for charging a penny above the state-controlled price on a box of matches, and had been arrested when she put up a fight? More pins in Nkrumah's hat coming to the surface . . . Did he know how many pins it took to deflate even his balloon? . . .

Woke up with a terrific ear ache this morning—full of fluid. Went to the hospital in Axim at the crack of dawn, only to find a long line of Ghanaian mothers with tons of babies strapped to their backs, clinging to their legs, or tucked comfortably in their arms, waiting to see if the "white man's doctor" could be successful where the village African doctor had failed.

Having no stomach for waiting under the already sizzling sun, I drove over to the nearby secondary school to see Sapp, a Barbadian teaching under contract with the Ghana government. Like most Afro-Americans in Ghana, the chap is pro-Nkrumah without reservations; yet, like many West Indians working in Ghana, he clings to the belief that his island is singularly free of racialism, even going so far as to credit the British colonial administration with having created this ideal society. Whenever I ask him why so many have run to Ghana, he merely looks puzzled.

On my return to Half Assini, I was dismayed to find that the school had no water—a situation that occurred all too frequently. So, back into the jeep and off to the beach for a dip (and only a dip, because I didn't know how to swim—the sad result of a childhood spent in a town where all nearby swimming pools were reserved for "whites only").

Lying under the shade of a coconut palm, I spied a seashell Armah had identified as one containing a dye used by local fishermen in their nets. When I had suggested that the dye probably afforded some protection against the corroding effects of the salty sea, Armah had merely laughed: "All you foreigners think that. The truth is that fetish priests believed it capable of assuring a good catch and of warding off any evil sea spirits that might be lurking in the ocean recesses to swallow boats and men." So much for my logical explanations!

Back at school, the local construction gang's road sprin-

kler was on. Ole Bos and I rushed to get our share of the dirty clay-colored water, our Ghanaian colleagues standing idly by, immersed in small talk while their apparently already overworked wives struggled to lug the heavy pails and pans into their kitchens. We obviously made an error in declining the students' offer to carry our buckets up the three flights of stairs, however, for we were greeted with hostile stares and heated murmurs. Not only do I prefer doing such things for myself; I refuse to be intimidated into a position merely to maintain an obviously British-imposed *status quo*.

I further displeased the students later in the day when I turned down their invitation to a party in honor of the principal. Ole Bos could put on a kente cloth (traditional dress) and go; as for me, there was too much symbolic meaning attached to the kente to allow for such prostitution of it. While sympathetic, the students nevertheless pointed out that, no matter how I worked at it, I was as much a product of American white society as Ole Bos, and if *he* could, *I* could. They just wouldn't see the difference, and left feeling dishonored by my stand.

Late in the evening it began to rain—barrelfuls poured out of the sky—but the sound couldn't drown out the strains of *Ghana, Guinea, Mali* coming in sweetly over Radio Ghana. I added a chorus of my own:

> Oh Ghana,
> The lone voice in the wilderness.
> Hold a steady course;
> Africa will someday answer . . .

MARCH 10

In class today I was greeted by the sight of several students parading around the room with white talcum-powder rings around one eye. I had noticed it on one other oc-

casion, but, knowing that any questions on my part would be interpreted as meddling, I had let it go. This time, however, one of the students brought it up, explaining that at certain times of the year certain people are required by custom to "deface" themselves in certain ways. I was to see white chalk or powder on many other Ghanaians, mostly elderly women, in the coming months whenever there was an important event.

But how the hell was I going to reach these kids if I couldn't even read the signs? Snooper that I am, I beat it over to one of the boys' dormitories after school and sought out the vice-prefect, second in command of student affairs. Soboe was a talkative chap and evidently more interested in politics than in customs; one of his uncles was a close associate of Dr. J. B. Danquah, opposition leader now awaiting trial in Ghana, who had fled to the Ivory Coast when the whip was cracked by the ruling party, and I had been told that Soboe planned to join him after graduation. (Now, there was true patriotism, African style!) So it was no surprise to me when I saw Gbedemah's *Ghanaians, Our True Freedom Must Be Won Now* on his desk. Mr. Gbedemah had been a former cabinet minister and close friend of the President's who had fled the country reportedly with thousands of pounds in currency, and initiated his own brand of opposition. I knew the pamphlet well: Gbedemah accuses Nkrumah and his party of betraying the original aims of the revolution, thereby relinquishing their claim to the loyalty and allegiance of the people. Further, he demands that those held in preventive detention be given a public trial (which indeed was being effected at this very moment). The United States is referred to by Mr. Gbedemah as that "bastion of real freedom." Why? Is he trying to win favor or does he already have it? I wouldn't be surprised if he and the other exiled opposition leader, Dr. K. A. Busia, already enjoyed our

covert support: wasn't Busia given the privilege to appear before Senator Dodd's committee? I considered telling Armah about it, but it certainly wouldn't do my relations with the students any good; no doubt others had this subversive document in their possession. Besides, perhaps even Armah wore a mask of loyalty . . .

But if I could learn nothing of these people's political beliefs by interfering, neither could I find many clues in Ghana's newspapers, most of which were incredibly dull, dogmatic, and totally lacking in appeal to the very Ghanaians to whom they are directed. Gwendolen Carter, in *Independent Africa,* cites the *Daily Graphic* (favorite of the masses) as an opposition paper, and I suspect that it was precisely because it enjoyed such popularity that the party recently purchased the tabloid, paying the owners, a London firm, a fair price.

One of my students, who was eager to pursue a political career, declared flatly that, were he Nkrumah, he would have acquired the *Daily Graphic* and all other opposition papers long ago; banned the opposition United party; and hung without trial the trio of former legislators now detained and presumably getting a fair trial, and all other bomb throwers and detractors. He cited the Russian example to illustrate how quickly and efficiently the state can handle thieves, defrauders, and other criminal elements, and was far from impressed when I tried to wiggle in a word about due process of law.

Though this kid had no great love for white Americans, he was determined to marry a white girl once he got to the States (and that he would get there was a foregone conclusion!). When I asked him why, he said bluntly, "To show off." Obviously, it had never occurred to him that he, with all his "political sophistication," was a prime example of what Ghanaian politicians meant when they used the term "colonial mentality"—one who, in his fight to

37

break the chains of his enslavement, confuses the means with the ends.

"Everybody should mix," he continued. Didn't a great Ghanaian freedom fighter (Dr. Aggrey) teach that, like the keys of a piano, blacks and whites must learn to pool their talents and work for the good of all—in all spheres of life?

Again and again I hear that old "Hess" refrain. (The Hesses spent one year here but quit the Corps when Mrs. got pregnant.) A fear of living among "ghosts and animals," as they so described their hosts, kept them from participating in all but necessary professional functions, a rejection that still rankles my students. Thus the colonial mentality works both ways: an uncritical acceptance of almost everything associated with the West can as easily turn to distrust in the face of real or imagined tormentors. An African girl can beg a white volunteer to have sexual relations with her for the sole purpose of "getting white babies"; while a student can attribute the demeaning nature of his punishment—crawling on hands and knees across the sidewalk—to the superiority the white man feels (in this case, Ole Bos). And, amazing as it seems, rarely is this subject discussed, even in academic and political circles, doubtless because of the emotion with which it is charged.

Speaking of distasteful subjects, I was finally asked to take my turn conducting the mandatory communal service for the school, a moment I'd been dreading. Damned if I'd fill those young impressionable minds with a lot of rot. Besides, I saw no reason why I should give a church service when I'd been barred from participating in Young Pioneer (the CPP youth wing) activities.

So, while students and faculty wrestled with the problem of a substitute preacher, I indulged in my favorite pastime: dropping coins down to the small fry. They really need it.

Little do they know that at this point I need it almost as much as they do: they must have cleaned me of fifteen bucks so far!

MARCH 11

Should have taught today but used my sore ear as an excuse to visit Accra. Ole Bos decided to come along. The Corps doctor there said it needed a rest. So did my head—was still trying to digest a morsel given me by one of the kids yesterday. It seems that Nkrumah conquered the rebellious Ashanti nation (seat of the notorious but now defunct National Liberation Movement) by transforming himself into a piece of bread, and thereby gaining entrance into NLM territory. That such news went unreported in leading scientific journals meant only that a select strata of individuals had access to the "truth," my student friend either being a member of that group or knowing one.

Well, whatever "magic" Nkrumah had worked in Ashantiland, his success would have to be measured against the fact that the Ashantis were then and are now ardent foes of the present regime.

I was to be confirmed in this opinion late in the afternoon by an American (not a PCV) who had recently arrived in Accra and was teaching political science at the University of Ghana. He had already conducted several informal surveys, and it seems that Nkrumah's success even in Ghana was open to debate: a large majority of the university's faculty, both foreign and domestic, had gripes about the President's "cult of personality," government expenditure on embassies and other foreign liabilities, and censorship of the press. The local papers, for example, carried no account of the recent incident at the Togo border: a group of Ghanaian university students bound for Nigeria's West African games was held six hours at the border,

39

and even Nkrumah's personal pleas to Togo's President didn't get them through. The beleaguered students had to turn around, return to Accra, and fly to Nigeria. A "violation" of air space is apparently not as repugnant as trespassing on land. At least there is less danger of contamination.

MARCH 12

The people in the Peace Corps office were beginning to think I was either homesick or coming down with a mild case of "cultural shock." They were right on both counts, but this particular morning I owed my gloominess to my blasted ear: this time because it wasn't serious enough to keep me in Accra. Damn!

Finally met Jill, the girl with the menstrual problem: the doc had curbed the flow and sent her back to her post in Togo, but the poor kid had to beat a hasty path back to Ghana after bleeding forty-eight hours without pause. Now, *there's* someone with problems—and I let a running ear push me 250 miles.

I'd do it again, too, without a drop of remorse, just for some good company. A day like today could drive me to it—only interesting part was my lunch with Abe and Ana (Harvard and Smith, PC marriage) and seeing their school. Buildings like tool sheds, dingy, dark, where the walls were so thin that teachers had to compete for whose voice was loud enough to get the kids' attention. They tell me that only five out of forty passed their certifying exams last year. I still see no reason to dispose of such schools, as has been suggested in some volunteer quarters. After all, a poor school is better than none! . . .

MARCH 14

Jill tells me that there are some in our group who call me

a racist—because I'm "so reserved and make no effort to be friendly" with our white element. Jesus, the irony of it! Were I white and aloof, I'd be just "another odd ball," but since I'm black, I'm necessarily a racist. Sure I'm discriminating—but not about color . . .

A little bit of hope: heard from Ole Bos (who's been staying with a friend) that the jeep won't be ready till Saturday. Bliss . . .

Thumbed a ride out to the university, that citadel of higher learning, where the foreigner strolls around in his Bermudas, the Ghanaian in his long woolen pants—despite the 100-degree heat! Never would the twain meet . . . as long as each conformed to a stereotype that even the civil servant had rejected (in favor of the more "American" and stylish long 'uns).

But if the university claimed this kind of African, bureaucracy attracted quite another: one who was going to enjoy his English legacy to the hilt. For every pimp and prisoner who had come out in the employ of the mother country and who could afford servants and chauffeurs, there would be an African to replace him and carry on the tradition of the chauffeured automobile. And why not? Surely Nkrumah's Ghana could allow for more than one interpretation of progress. And progress it was: modern buildings going up everywhere, roads laid, new hospitals, schools, shipping lines, harbors; people wearing expensive clothes, driving Pontiacs, Mercedes-Benzes . . . Granted that many still have to walk some distance to collect water from public pumps; just a few years ago there were no pumps to walk *to*. Those who would oppose Nkrumah's government while reaping the benefits of such technological advances might be wise to consider the millions of poverty-stricken individuals in the United States—a *land of plenty*—who are in many cases worse off than the Ghanaian who still works a meager farm. I would much rather be a broke and full-stomached (even on a starch diet)

41

peasant than a broke *and* hungry *and* abandoned slum dweller.

> Live on, proud Ghana
> Detractors, nay
> Create for Africa
> A shining beacon the world to gaze on
> A new Africa, a new African . . .

MARCH 15

Went up to the girls' floor and did a little romancing . . . find it pleasantly annoying that Jill sometimes forgets her sex and leaves everything up. It's not *that* hot . . . She too thinks that marrying white is to the African what owning a Cadillac and a luxury home is to the American Negro. What a sorry mess that even here in Ghana, a country claimed by black men as their own, black people still think only white skin is worthy of respect, dignity, and pride. Wasn't it DuBois who said that we fail to see within ourselves the same flowers of beauty and genius manifest in all of mankind everywhere? "Everybody is rich but me" . . .

MARCH 16

Jackie, a volunteer in a large western city, was the first of the usual weekend horde to arrive at the hostel, and though my bubble of bliss was beginning to tear at the seams, I took her and Jill to a local movie. The audience, unlike those high-salaried Ghanaians and Europeans who always went downtown, put on a better show, alternately hissing and cheering whenever the villain got his. They even mimicked the punching, occasionally hitting each other, but no one seemed to mind.

From the movie, we taxied over to the Metropole, a pop-

ular night club frequented largely by Indians and Europeans. It could have been a club in Alabama, the way they stared! A black man with two white girls? Why didn't we go to the Lido, where *that* sort of thing went on all the time . . . Why not indeed? Screw them!

The Lido, Ghana's most popular club, was really rocking when we got there. Danced till the joint closed, then, dropping Jackie at the hostel and picking up a couple of Canadians, went for an early morning dip in the Atlantic. Jill watched us from a shallow foxhole she had dug in the sand. She's the greatest—paid for the whole evening, slipping money into my palm as we downed beer after beer at the clubs . . .

MARCH 17

My bubble burst: the horde from the bush arrived and Jesus, what a crush! But I was glad to see a guy I hadn't seen since we took off for our separate assignments, Bob War, a native Mississippian who had to come to Ghana to learn that black's a beautiful color and his family name a source of pride (being of Ghanaian derivation and one of the few to be carried to the States).

His village is lucky enough to have a secondary school: although very small—only a few hundred people—it remained, even during the NLM hostilities, one of the few Ashanti towns unreservedly pro-Nkrumah. Yet few students want to attend a school so far from any sizable town, and few teachers are willing to move their families to such an intellectually arid community. Bob says teaching there is frustrating as hell, but he has come to the conclusion that, no matter how problematical, such schools are worthwhile, if only because they reflect Nkrumah's determination for progress in Ghana and, ultimately, for African continental unity. (I was amused later, when I happened

43

to glance through Bob's racing form, to see evidence of this drive even in the names of the horses! African Personality, Great Ghana, The Sixth of March, Black Boy, Ghana Solidarity, Young Pioneer . . .)

This was also to be the last day Jill and I would see each other, perhaps for a very long time: we were heading home tomorrow. I had really grown quite fond of her in the short time we'd been together, but I'm hell on good-byes, so we took in a movie and then made it to the hostel roof, where we talked until the stars blinked out in the dawn. Somehow everything's less complicated in the clear, fresh beginning of a morning . . .

MARCH 18

Ole Bos and I left Accra for our bush home with the jeep still in various degrees of disrepair. Gave Jackie a lift to Salt Pond, where we spent a miserable hour in heated discussion with two volunteer friends of hers. Like others I had met in the past few months, they were opposed to the Ghana Young Pioneers, but, when pressed for details, they clammed up. The girl mumbled something about the girls in her school being stupid, anyway. No doubt she thought they ought to go back to the trees, too . . . What the hell could any teacher expect of girls who for generations have been taught that education is for men; that the woman's place is at the home, looking after her kids and obeying her husband? And how could this girl's fiance expect Ghanaian male students to perform mechanical tasks with the adeptness of American kids when many of them have never even seen a screwdriver before?

But then they weren't so different from teachers I knew back in the States who worked with "culturally deprived" kids . . . Every now and then a rough contempt broke through to permanently scar that flawless surface. What

really troubles me is the thought that all volunteers are having more than some difficulty accepting their children at *whatever* level of achievement they find them, and—even sadder—seeing Ghana through the hopes and aspirations of Ghanaian eyes.

We left Jack and Jill's cute little bungalow in a cloud of dust and disappointment. Westward ho! Felt like a city boy who is forced to live on the farm. Back to the grit and grind. As Ole Bos and I neared the ferry, a young man rushed out of the nearby forest waving frantically to us and pleading for a ride to Esiama, that relic of yesteryear's gold-rush days: his father had just died. We agreed to drop him as close to his village as we could.

The young man was withdrawn, quiet, until we reached the ferry, but at that moment, struck by the full impact of his loss, he began to sob. A slight figure, chanting lamentations, nose running . . . Everybody on the ferry watched in silence, eyes large with concern, pity. Only the ferry tender chanted along with him. Long-buried memories suddenly welled up in me as I tried to be brave and keep face —almost overcome by my own drive for compassion, for I, too, knew the bitter sting of personal loss, emptiness . . . It would seem that "ghosts and animals" had at least one human quality after all . . .

I was never able to find out whether it had actually been the young man's father who had died: in matrilineal societies like that of the Nzima, the mother's eldest brother traditionally assumes the role of father, whereas in patrilineal groups the line of descent is traced through the natural father.

MARCH 19

I set a personal precedent last night by going to communal service, where, without previous intent, I gave an im-

45

promptu speech on "Africa and Others." The words just seemed to spring out of an inner necessity; after what I had heard during the past week, I felt compelled to tell my students that if they wished to be accepted as equals in a world riddled with inequality, they had to work hard to project an image that would not lend itself to such terms as *monkeys, dark continent, animals, savages,* and *ghosts.*

Then, for some reason unknown even to me, I tackled the catch-all political term *neo-colonialism.* (Perhaps it was my desire to include Americans in that list of "others.") When Ghana, according to rumors, threatened to demand withdrawal of all foreign teachers of African history, the U.S. ambassador promised to withdraw all teachers—and suspend work on the huge Volta Dam. We stayed. Then, only last week, a volunteer was reassured by a Peace Corps official that should she be asked to leave the country because of her anti-Young Pioneer attitude, all volunteers would be unilaterally withdrawn. Now, if these aren't examples of neo-colonialist tactics, somebody had better clue me in in a hurry . . .

The kids seemed to be taking it all in, and after I had finished and the others had gone home, a student from Accra came up to me with a novel request (perhaps to see how far he could trust *this* American's attitudes!). A *ju ju* (magic) man in Accra had asked the student to request from me fare to Half Assini as payment for services he could render, like doubling any amount of money I wished. Sounded like the old con game to me; but, out of curiosity and in deference to the kid's wishes, I took a rain check. He then asked if I would be afraid to accompany the *ju ju* man to a cemetery at midnight. I said no, but then, without thinking, quoted the old American cliché—"only the living can harm the living." My young friend shot me an angry look—ancestor worship holds an honored place in the lives of many Africans—and, realizing my error, I

46

quickly added that even if the dead could communicate with the living, the *ju ju* man would surely protect me. He looked relieved.

Incidentally, this student has been warned by his father —a high-ranking CPP official—to stay away from the Young Pioneers, since it's nothing more than a propagandist outfit. What kills me is that this man, formerly a member of the United party, is now responsible for the CPP's entire *propaganda* program!

Random thoughts: The entire staff of the local elementary school was flabbergasted when I delivered the books I had ordered from London. I let them think it was the Peace Corps and not I alone who was their benefactor (but damned if I would ever ask for them back!).

. . . Kojo Bostio, demoted some time ago for mishandling state funds, reappointed as Ghana's Foreign Minister. He had played it cool, waiting for this moment to be reinstated.

. . . Heard over the BBC that South Africa is now considered part of the "free world." Them and *their* "free world" . . .

M A R C H   2 0

Will wonders never cease? Today the school messenger handed me a letter from a Ghanaian colleague (Allah-Mensah) in which he accuses me of flirting with his wife. "And," the letter continues, "if you were a Ghanaian, I would know what drastic steps to take." Ghanaians, it seems, have a rather formal way of voicing complaints— the fellow lived only two floors below me—but I was later told that, in matters of importance, it was a common practice to write rather than speak to those concerned. After some consideration, I sent my friend a return letter in which he was invited to ignore my nationality and to

47

consider the fact that my contract with the Peace Corps included no provision for seduction. Furthermore, I added, it would seem down right self-defeating to see bestial motives behind every smile of greeting: think of how many letters one would have to write, how many "drastic steps" . . .

And only a few hours before, I had been accused of an even greater indiscretion. I was chatting amiably with Young Man Morkek, called by *Drum* (Africa's *Ebony*) "The Uncrowned King of Half-Assini" for his tireless efforts to improve the town, and the resident foreign-affairs official, when suddenly the old man stopped in mid-sentence, turned a bony finger at me, and began to yell. How dare I not believe in God (a tale he had got from the town news vendor, one who, being a devout Christian—in fact, a Jehovah's Witness—scrambled to report this breach of faith to his master). Worse still, how dare I talk about it? And, my mouth still agape, I was warned in no uncertain terms never again to say such things if I wanted my stay to be enjoyable and profitable. "God" just happens to be a topic we finite humans don't go around questioning, even for intellectual exercise, as I had lamely excused my blunder.

After which the foreign-affairs representative, finding this a suitable occasion to let off some steam of his own (fortunately not at me), launched into a vitriolic monologue about Half Assini's lack of social amenities and intellectual stimulation. Nothing to do, and no one ever comes across the Ghana-Ivory Coast border on subversive missions. His one hope was that Bostio would help an old crony and call him back to Accra, where he had spent twenty-five years among the political brass. Even he, an Nzima, could not escape the "stranger" tag pinned to all from beyond the veil.

I didn't know which was more serious: being accused of blasphemy or seduction. But at least Morkek rested his case then and there: the letter affair was still on the docket, as I learned a few hours later. The principal had called a meeting of the Management Committee and assigned certain faculty members—all Ghanaians—to deal with the charge made against me. Both my letter and Allah-Mensah's had already been burned when he summoned me to his office. They had no intention of "prosecuting," he said, the matter would be kept under the rug, but I was never to forget that any man not a personal friend of the African husband's who touches his wife or even looks at her too long can expect a knock in the snooch. This restriction never applies to the husband's personal friends, who, as one juror laughingly pointed out, can occupy the wife's bed and never know a raised brow from the husband, who knows that "ain't nothing happening."

As I left the meeting, my only thought was that a change of pace was desperately needed, or I might wind up at Ackah's *ju ju* man with a headache of my own . . .

MARCH 21

The rain has come and gone, leaving literally thousands of mosquitoes to buzz their discontent: but I am content in my netted bed . . . catnapping . . . Radio German Democratic Republic coming in loud and clear . . . What must be East Germany's version of Tokyo Rose putting in her bit about the lack of racial discrimination in her country . . . Doesn't she know that Africans consider almost any other problem more pressing than discrimination? That Ghanaians couldn't care less about racial turmoil in "imperialist" America? That most Africans returning from schools in her land of equality don't share her enthusiasm for communism's answer to racism?

49

Radio Ghana External now . . . fire and brimstone:

Fellow Freedom Fighters
Cooperation between African and non-African workers
Sons and daughter of the soil
Join no blocs.

Workers of Africa unite
Nothing to lose but your chains
Carry on the fight, Freedom Fighters.

Long live African workers
Long live African Unity
Long live African Freedom Fighters . . .

How many Angolan mothers are fervently listening to those words? How many fighters in the field? . . .

A pestering head cold is still going strong as ever, fever burning me up. A bottle of hot cedar and Ghana Gin No. 1 will either knock it out or knock me out of it.

Am now watching a flock of white egrets flying over the soccer field. They usually stay close to the compound, working over freshly cut grass. Unlike the ubiquitous vultures, egrets won't allow man within twenty-five yards or so. Rather jumpy creatures. But just as graceful in flight as the crows along the seashore at twilight . . .

MARCH 22

Learned today from a contractor friend that Ackah has just authorized the building of a tennis court. Probably still reaching out in desperation for student favor. Believed it even more when I pulled this old wreck of a body out of bed and lurched over to see how the boys were doing. Few were studying; most were playing Monopoly or other games—another gift from Ackah.

It was a hard fight, but temptation finally won out over

reason, and I wobbled into town on my *ju ju* cane. I still find it amusing that many of my friends there can't believe that I'm a bachelor, and, worse, that I don't even have a lover. It's not natural, they say, and I agree! But willing dames are few and too far between in bush villages, what with most fellows taking two or three and drying up the supply. Whether or not the practice of polygamy is hard for the woman, it sure works against unfortunate guys like me.

Returning to the compound half high and buoyant in spirit, I ambled over to Ackah's quarters and reiterated my desire to transfer, even though "I have much respect and veneration for your people the Nzima." My request for a transfer had not been acted upon, he was quick to reply, because he really wanted to keep me and ship out Ole Bos. He even said that he had in his possession a "confidential" report in which the Deputy Minister of Education was opposed to white volunteers teaching African history but didn't mind Afros teaching it. (That I had more "feeling" than Ole Bos I didn't doubt, but later I was to discover that no such report had ever been issued by the Minister.)

MARCH 23

What a dreary early morn. Quiet as the stalking hunter of snakes in an even quieter forest, except for the oink-oinks of wild boars and occasional beep beeps of restless owls . . . Rolling thunder in the distance . . . A downpour was on its way. What's annoying is that one never knows the direction from which the rain will come; if I had left my windows open, as they were before some *ju ju* man advised me to close them, my bedroom would have been a raging sea.

Got request for transfer off to Deputy Minister of Education, copies to Peace Corps and several teacher-training

schools. Broke Corps code by writing directly to Ministry. Will catch hell from Boss Carter but, dammit, I'm fed up with Ackah's stalling.

It poured off and on all day, but I made it over to police barracks for a short visit with Armah and several of his friends. He gave me a watch as a gesture of "black brotherhood." Said that if I lost it, our bond was broken. Seemed sincere enough, but what a flimsy foundation on which to claim ancestral ties: a cheap Hausa trader import with a life span designed to discourage that very brotherhood.

What did I think of Nkrumah now? he suddenly asked, with a gleam in his eye. A grenade explodes just a few feet from where the man is standing, and he walks away without a scratch! Surely even *I* had to admit he has mystical powers after all.

It was indeed miraculous, but I couldn't help thinking that, had Nkrumah belonged to a tribe other than Armah's and escaped unhurt, a more rational explanation would have been offered: "He was shielded by those around him"; or, "He *was* injured badly but the public wasn't informed."

I didn't dare say this aloud, however, because I didn't want to get into a hassle over something as nebulous as how many lives a cat has. I'd much rather feel them out on something more concrete and with every bit as much meaning for them (if they would only see it). They were always more than willing to talk about the oppression of the African at the hands of the European overseer, but I wasn't so sure they saw in the plight of the Negro in America that very same kind of oppression, nor even considered "racial injustice" at the core of both. I was right. It was "political" or "economic" expedience that moved the colonialist to behave the way he did: thus it must be the same with the Afro-American and *his* master in the States. That "racial injustice" had philosophical and psycho-social implications just didn't occur to them—mainly because they

saw discrimination in purely personal terms. It's like a Negro in Alabama who hears stories of lynchings and bombings, or actually sees brutalities inflicted on his brothers by whites, and says "They didn't do it to me, *I'm* not oppressed. *They* are." So with Armah and his pals. Yes it *was* horrible about the Negro in the States, they had no idea *how* bad until I told them, but what did it have to do with them? The Afro-American would some day liberate himself the way they had, and everything would be all right, wouldn't it? No it wouldn't, I said, because for the black man to be really free, he must have the world's respect for his identity *as a black man*—an identity that can be forcefully stated only when black men everywhere take on each other's struggle for their own. There is only one fight to be fought, I said, and it can't be won if Troop A doesn't know what the hell Troop B is doing, or doesn't care.

They looked at me as if I had gone mad—and perhaps I had. But I comforted myself with the thought that one day they might remember my words—the day the black man no longer had to justify his existence to anyone, most of all himself.

What with all the admonishments by PC training officials, PC Washington, and PC field staff, volunteers generally keep a tight lip regarding Ghana's political affairs, but, since little of an apolitical nature happens around here, I'll be damned if I'll be intimidated any more. Out with the newspaper clippings I collected in February! Old news is better than no news . . . maybe. First item reveals that at this time last year, Ghana's President wasn't nearly as vociferous and urgent in his demands for African political unity, and people like Nigeria's Belawa weren't pushing it either, but for different reasons: they thought Nkrumah was out for the whole African pie for himself.

Second interesting item: an ad for a book by George

Padmore, West Indian advisor on African affairs to Nkrumah until his untimely and universally mourned death, that has been running in the *Ghanaian Times* for months; yet, when I asked if they knew of the book, nine out of ten in Half Assini said no. That they haven't bothered to educate politically those in the bush areas could be a serious oversight on the part of the CPP. I don't think the woman who overcharged me on a box of matches would have done so if she had known why it is to her interests, as well as to others', to keep prices stable.

A third item—"Kwame Meets Mary"—brings to mind a remark dropped by one of the locals the other day, that the President has made few public appearances of late, and not because, as the papers claim, important foreign guests are keeping him busy. "It's the bombings," he said. "He's *afraid* to give speeches out in the open, now, so he has his aides do it." From what I can gather, this guy speaks for a large number of Nkrumah's followers, who are suddenly beginning to wonder why he doesn't give them even a little peek at that Osagyefo "who never dies." Why doesn't he use his *ju ju,* transform himself into a piece of bread again so that he can move among his people? Or is he afraid of being eaten this time?

Now that the "enemies of the people" are on trial, charges and counter-charges are being thrown about like so many balls in a juggling act. Accused accusing the presumed innocent; old party associates claiming never to have known each other. Present ministers and old party bosses Krobo Edusi, Ofori-Atta, Kwaku Boateng alike all under fire from certain elements of the party *and* the detained. One wonders who takes these charges seriously, however, for it is well known that Mr. Edusi is in Tokyo on an agricultural mission with the blessings of the Party; and Justice Minister Ofori-Atta just delivered the President's prepared speech to delegates at

54

the Local Authority Conference. Boateng is the only one not accounted for, but I wouldn't be surprised if he was having lunch with the Boss right now.

One last point of interest: the *Graphic,* apparently feeling the whip of either party or conscience, has finally dropped its daily "European only" job ads . . . I wonder if they'll adopt that old Chicago subterfuge when "white only" ads were forced to go: a discreet telephone tip from employment agency to employer, a special coding system designating race . . .

MARCH 24

Though our training at Berkeley had touched on "matrilineal societies," and though I knew the Nzima was such an example, it was only today that I really saw the system at work (or rather, *not* at work) . Most of the teachers at Half Assini could send their children to be reared by their wives' elder brothers. Not the English prof. He was a "modern" believer and had refused to burden his brothers-in-law with his wife's children. But as far as his own burden was concerned, refusal to accept his sister's children would automatically reap scorn, abuse, and ridicule not only on him but on his relatives, and should he at some point in the future desire the services of his wife's brothers, he would find them none too receptive. So there he was with a whole slew of kids to support and all because he was a "sophisticate."

It's a joy to learn that the young boys had been saving the pennies I've been giving them: one is strutting around in a pair of smart new school pants. We are both proud, he because he no longer has to wear tattered rags and submit to the heckling of more fortunate schoolmates, and I because such a small gesture could produce such happiness. But I'm appalled at the ten-shilling cost of the

trousers; not more than a month ago the CPP announced a reduction of six shillings for school uniforms. Either the news hasn't reached the bush yet, or the market women are overcharging again.

Neither of these two boys belongs to the Young Pioneers: their uncle and provider is something of a model Christian and preaches on occasion to the local Methodist church. His opposition to the Organization is, therefore, quite in keeping with the conservative and often outright reactionary views held by the missionary element in Ghana.

MARCH 25

This morning seemed as good a time as any to start asking students to fill out a questionnaire I had been designing for some months. As I anticipated, they were somewhat nervous about my motives. I carefully explained that this was a common tool of educators interested in their pupils, and that I had no intention of revealing the contents to the "wrong people." Besides, they were not required to sign their names.

It took me a while to convince them of my sincerity, however: they were still smarting under the blow dealt them by the Hesses.

Unfortuunately, Ackah caught me just as I was distributing the papers to the third class. I was quick to assure him that no school money or material was involved, I had financed the project out of my own pocket; but he snatched up a copy and stalked away, scowling and muttering to himself.

At 3:30 P.M. I was handed the following letter:

25-3-63

Dear Mr. Smith,

I have read through the list of questions you gave me

this morning, and I must confess I am not happy at all about it. If you had shown it to me before seeking answers from the students, I would not have allowed you to do so. For the nature of the questions is such that I will be black-listed if any Intelligence Officer or Government official hears of it.

The procedure you passed through was wrong. I am afraid, as things are in Ghana at present, I shall have to make this known to the D.C. [the District Commissioner]. I know for certain that the Government of Ghana will not tolerate this, whether it comes from a Peace Corps Master, or an Overseas Master, or an African Master.

Meanwhile, please surrender all answer sheets forthwith.

March 1963

HALF ASSINI SECONDARY SCHOOL

Please be truthful. Ask questions if you don't understand.

1. Your age _____ 2. Form _____ 3. Male _____ Female _____
4. Home town _____ Is your home town in eastern Nzima? _____ western Nzima? _____ Other? _____
5. Have you been sick this academic year? _____ How many times? _____ What was the illness? _____
6. What will you do upon completing secondary school?_____
7. What is your favorite newspaper? _____
8. What country would you like to visit or study in? First choice _____ 2nd _____ 3rd _____
9. What is your father's occupation? _____ Your mother's? _____
10. Have you always lived in the same town? _____ What other towns have you lived in for more than a year? _____ _____, _____, _____
11. How many living brothers do you have? ___ Sisters? ___ How many brothers are dead? _____ Sisters? _____ How many brothers in school? _____ Sisters? _____
12. Have you visited Accra? _____ Takoradi? _____ Kumasi? _____ Tamale? _____

57

13. What countries outside of Ghana have you visited? _____
    Do you have relatives in other countries? _____ Which
    country or countries? _____
14. What school subject do you like best? _____
    Least?_____
15. What newspaper do you *enjoy* reading? _____
16. In what school subject do you get your best marks? _____
17. In what town or city do you hope to live after completing
    your secondary schooling? _____
18. To what youth group or organization do you belong? ___
19. What languages do you speak? _____
20. Who is your best friend in school? _____
    Which student do you like the least? _____
21. If you were given a choice, which secondary school would
    you like to attend? _____
22. Who is your favorite master? _____
23. From what master are you learning the most? _____
24. What job or occupation do you hope to enter upon com-
    pletion of *all* your schooling?

With a mixture of disgust and fear, I immediately went
to Ackah's office, where I went over the thing item by
item, drawing comparisons with a copy of a similar but
more sophisticated survey conducted by *Ghanaian* pro-
fessors at the University of Ghana. All to no avail!

Now came the crucial test: I'd have to find out how
successful or unsuccessful my public relations had been
with the villagers. Big men first. The District Commissioner surreptitiously examined both documents and
promised to "hear my case" the following morning at the
regular meeting of the school's Board of Governors.

A little disappointed, I walked around the corner to the
post office and sought out my friend the postmaster, one
with whom I had shared many laughs and for whom I had
a good deal of respect. He expressed open surprise that
"subversion" could be read into my questionnaire, but

quickly added that such happenings were rather common around the school. In fact, he himself had been charged by my principal's predecessor with attempting to incite riots and strikes among the students. I was beginning to feel better: at least I wasn't alone in this experience.

Armah, the next person I saw, and one who should certainly be an expert in such matters, suggested that the principal was off his rocker, but was a little miffed that I hadn't told him of my intention beforehand. The clerk of council shared Armah's opinion and promised to exert his influence as a member of the Board in my favor.

MARCH 2 6

Woke up with a splitting headache—and a galloping case of anxiety. How could I win against that guy, given the extent of his tribal ties with the members of the Board?

I considered writing a formal letter to the Board but decided against it: the Peace Corps would probably split a gut. The school bursar, who had also had his share of problems—he was accused but never "tried" for pocketing school monies—advised me to bide my time and, above all, be discreet: a new principal was on the way.

I waited on tenterhooks until 1:30 P.M., when, finally, I was summoned to the hearing. As I made my way over to the school, I was suddenly overcome by a terrific desire to run. I should have: the board, with the aid of the Regional Education Officer, had reached a verdict of guilty. No, they would not hear the defendant's case. He would receive a formal notification of their decision, but, in the meantime, was to surrender to the principal all questionnaires, including those filled in.

I suppose I should have been grateful that I was guilty, not of engaging in subversive activities but only of failing to consult the principal before embarking on the project.

59

But I was angrier than hell. The Board had given its final statement on the matter—there would be no reconsideration of its decision—and that was that!

The crowning idiocy of the whole affair struck me as I was leaving the teachers' lounge to fetch the papers: there in the corridor, nervously pacing back and forth and obviously pondering over the mysterious happenings in the adjoining room, was the principal-to-be. They had denied him the right to sit in, even as an observer, on my trial!

I took my woes to a friend in the Ministry of Foreign Affairs: if anyone could help me, *he* could. My macabre description of "academic freedom" and humanitarian justice didn't fall on deaf ears. Pounding his fists on the desk and snorting loudly, he vowed that he would take the matter to Accra, claim undue and dangerous harassment, and not only demand an apology but insist that my papers be returned.

My spirits soared: given a clean bill of health by a representative of the government, surely my survey would at least escape the torch. I raced to Ackah's office, feeling gutsier than I had in weeks, but, not finding him, went back to my friend, this time with a copy in hand. I was to curse myself for this moment of bravado, for, after reading it carefully, his tune changed. Whatever one writes or says will be interpreted in light of the observer's occupation, his attitudes toward the writer, and his own experience . . . The boom was about to fall . . . Thus, the *implications* of certain items on the questionnaire would catch the eye of an alert intelligence officer. Further, were it not for our friendship, and his certainty as to the purity of my motives, he himself would be as alarmed as the principal and make similar accusations! Man, what a world—up, down, all around, you put your left foot in, you take your left foot out . . .

One must exercise great caution, he continued, even when sympathetic to the progressive forces of the African revolution as defined and realized in Ghana. Item 8, for example—name the foreign country you would most like to visit or study in—could, under certain circumstances and evaluated by certain people, be construed as a method for determining candidates for subversion. Items 7 and 15 could determine the popularity, or lack of it, of the party press; and item 18 could seriously undermine the efforts of the party's youth wing to build a strong and viable nationalist youth movement.

He further suggested that it was not necessarily *my* motives, but those of the Peace Corps as an intelligence network, that were suspect. Volunteers had access to certain kinds of information that might be of interest and use to the CIA. After all, didn't *I* know that Ghanaian troops had moved by night to the Ivory Coast border during the attempted *coup* in that country? And didn't I know that certain of my older students had acted as messengers for exiled Ghanaian opposition leaders? Under these circumstances, he continued, 125 volunteers—visiting other countries, meeting with top officials, communicating their observations to God knows who—could well be considered an extension—even if amateurish—of the CIA. Thus his final advice to me was to go very politely to the principal and, on my own initiative, ask that all copies be burned in his presence.

To further confuse matters, when I saw the Education Officer later, *he* stated quite openly that, as an instrument of education, the survey was the shot in the arm the school needed, and would have been a credit both to his office and to the school's reputation. As far as he was concerned, the principal had acted rashly and would probably be willing to return the papers if only to end the whole nasty mess.

61

I was dizzy with exhilaration again . . . but not for long.
I remembered the case of the German road engineer who
on his off day, had gone around taking innocent photos of
the wrecked ship on the beach (simply because the wreck
had become famous as a landmark used by Nkrumah to
estimate his age) and the President's nearby beach house,
and was immediately arrested and preliminarily charged
with attempting to get the layout (possibly for sabo-
tage?) of the area. What if Washington were to be involved in my case, as Bonn had been in the engineer's?

MARCH 27

First thing this morning we stood at the funeral pyre,
Ackah and I, and watched my one strong effort go up
in smoke. Another day in the life of a Peace Corps Volunteer in Ghana . . .

Life goes on as before. Just had biology class. Boys
can't wait till we get around to reproduction: want to
know about "that bone in the penis." Girls, as usual, very
quiet on the subject.

Gnawing feeling still inside. How the hell can I be of
any help in the reconstruction of Africa if my hands are
tied? My friend of the Foreign Ministry tells me I can't—at
least not here, where ignorance breeds distrust . . . Where,
then? Shall I go home and send CARE packages that they
don't need so they know I CARE? Jesus . . .

MARCH 28

Just spent a couple of hours with Rocky, a British Guin-
ean who is building what the press describes as a rest
house for weary travelers and tourists. He can't understand why such a remote site was chosen: how did they
expect to make a dime? Well, maybe they didn't . . .

Not so long ago, during the Ivory Coast crisis, that area was jumping with tanks, artillery, mortars, and about five companies of infantry.

Ole Bos returned from a visit to the Ivory Coast today, laden with several bottles of excellent—but contraband— French wine. He consented to give me three, but with the proviso that I pick mine up from that rabid racist African-hating priest. I appropriated the three bottles he forgot to remove from the jeep. He was furious, accused me of insulting his integrity. Well, well, well . . . the guy's not *altogether* blind!

MARCH 29

Had a rotten experience in class today and committed an unpardonable blunder. One of my students was concentrating on something other than his biology text, and for some strange reason I felt gravely threatened by this show of disrespect. I stopped in mid-sentence, turned an icy glare on the kid, and put it to him bluntly: either join the class or take the book and read it elsewhere. He didn't budge; neither did he put the book away. I threatened to deposit him bodily on the sidewalk. "You are capable of doing no such thing," he said quietly, keeping his gaze steady. I drew in a deep breath, waited, stalling for time. The students watched me intently. Would I carry out my threat? . . . Turn the whole thing into a joke? . . .

Idiot that I was, I could do neither, so I stalked out of the room, depriving the whole class of their lesson. I comforted myself with the thought that in the future they might not *let* a student interfere with their education. But whose was that burden really? I was copping out, and both they and I knew it . . .

Just learned through the grapevine that Bob War is on a plane for home: So much for my expert analyses! And

63

I thought he had finally seen the light (or perhaps I should say "the dark!").

MARCH 30

The damn principal must be having fits of schizophrenia. Just two days after he accuses me of being a threat to the security of the school, he tells me he can have Ole Bos shipped out, and I won't have to transfer. What the hell makes him think pasty face bugs me *that* much?

MARCH 31

Rocky dropped by rather unexpectedly last night and persuaded me to accompany him to a dance in Esiama, at a hotel owned by some of the big party boys. I don't know why I let him; it was just the way I thought it would be—lousy. The big boys in a huge banquet room they had taken for their pleasure; and to be separated from the "proletariat," "the wave of the future," in whom they say they have so much faith. Rocky and I silently cursing the hypocrites, and drowning our depression with the more realistic bank officials who had long ago abandoned their illusions about the benevolence of their political fathers. They no longer, except as an expedient to save a job or wangle a favor from an official, mouthed slop slogans.

But the party wouldn't be complete until a guy with a million-dollar sales grin implored "the American to get him to the States," which he did and which I point-blank refused to do—a sour note on which to end a perfectly sour evening.

APRIL 2

I wonder how many new faces will appear with Ackah's

64

replacement. The last time a principal left, the school lost half its teaching staff and a good number of students as well. That tribes stick together here is not really as different from what groups of people do anywhere when confronted with momentous decisions. Even in rural Alabama, when civil rights workers disagreed on courses of action, relatives, members of a leader's church, and old school chums were often the determinants of final decisions. And, more often than not, a leader was chosen on grounds other than his qualifications, i.e., how strong a member of the in-group he was, where he lived, etc. So . . . not chauvinism but the less sophisticated concept of people needing to relate in a meaningful way with other human beings explains (and indeed justifies) the direction loyalty takes. In vital matters, it becomes outsider versus insider, the former constantly threatening the latter's sense of reality. And what defines the outsider sometimes seems totally arbitrary: perhaps he is a member of a different class or community, or belongs to a different church, race or civil rights organization. Exclusiveness, it seems, belongs to the world . . .

The kids who entered the science competition returned from the national meet today. What a thrill for me! We won first and third place. Well, brother Ackah, and you didn't think we were ready! *Your* problem . . .

American students are not alone in possessing the "capitalist mentality." Played several hours of Monopoly with some of the students, and couldn't place higher than third!

Exams are coming up. Students in latrines, under beds, sprawled under coconut trees chewing lessons. They're quick to deny that they're absorbed in memorizing the material, but we all laugh, because in Ghana, learning by rote is the one method that insures success. The technique is as old as Ghana's education system itself and

65

earns a badge of merit for those who are most adept at
it.

Ole Bos seems to be coming down with a severe case of
Volunteer jitters: blew up at his houseboy, John, for nothing other than using his gas stove without permission—
even threatened to fire him. The kid was in tears.

Got a letter from Boss Carter spewing fire and brimstone at me for having written to the Deputy Minister
of Education requesting a transfer. What infuriated him
was not that I wanted to leave, but that I had broken
company regulations, which, in no uncertain terms, for-
bid volunteers from going directly to the Ministry for anything. He would try to patch things up—*this* time. Boy,
did he patch things up! . . .

APRIL 3

Wild pigs on the prowl tonight. First time they have
seemed so close. Hunters will be out setting traps and
blasting off with their ancient shotguns and muskets.
Writing by candlelight: no electricity after 10 P.M.

One of my kids came to me today and asked if he could
"go take a shit." To know how to use such expressions insures a kid's popularity, makes him one of the "guys."
That these terms are considered vulgar and impertinent
by the very people from whom they were learned, Americans, never occurred to these kids, whose only concern is
to conform as closely as possible to their conception of the
model American teen-ager.

While in town to pick up the science prizes at the Regional Education Office, I bumped into Ocran, the District Organizer for the Young Pioneers. He tells me that
a new regional party building is in the works, and each
district within the region is expected to raise 1,000 pounds.
The District Commissioner at Nkroful, Nkrumah's birth

place, has already raised far more than the required amount, while the D.C. here, strutting from village to village in his Western-cut suit, carrying a *ju ju* stick, has still to get a nickel. The President has ordered all D.C.'s to attend a series of seminars directed at "giving them an ideology": too many of them are more interested in their own tribes than in the CPP.

A P R I L 4

Well, Half Assini becomes a part of the national commercial effort. The Ghana National Trading Corporation (GNTC), a privately financed but state-controlled enterprise, is setting up shop in town. Had it not been for Morkek, *the* local merchant of means, all stores in Half Assini would be the property of the government. As it is, Morkek was allowed to put up the capital and, as a reward, was given the option of putting his own clerks in charge. To avoid death by competition, his GNTC store would sell only those items not available in his other thriving shops. Thus he retains decisive control over the goods in *all* the stores while reaping a nice profit from his private one—as long as the government boys don't start wondering why he never sells certain items in the GNTC store. An "old" (seventy-five to eighty-five) man thinking and acting young.

An elaborate and annoying bookkeeping system insures the government its cut, and a government auditor makes regular checks to make sure the dealer keeps his paws out of the till. Not capitalism, not private enterprise, either, but an apparently effective cross between them and "pure" socialism.

Tonight I attended the Ghanaian bush variety of a musical concert. To the "foreigner" they are at best noisy, loud, and fast: not knowing the vernacular, he misses

all the jokes. But to the Ghanaian they are the high spot of the week.

Sex is a favorite theme, and, as Ghanaians are free from the fetters of the Puritan ethic, the skits are liberally sprinkled with such words as *urine, penis,* and *intercourse* —guaranteed to draw hearty laughter from the audience.

The performers, usually amateur musician-actors, leave no body movement untested in their efforts to capture all eyes and ears. Remarkably resembling our more active rock-and-roll groups, the musicians play their guitars while reclining on the floor, kneeling, and even standing on their heads! The audience, wildly enthusiastic, showers the stage with coins, candy, and anything else they might have in their pockets.

During the first act of this particular show, the audience —including even this bemused soul—collapsed with laughter at the appearance of a character with white-painted lips and a padded groin: oversized testicles. For a more dramatic effect he had even smoothed charcoal dust over his ebony-hued skin. Totally different in tone and spirit, the second act was meaty, with all sorts of political implications. An old gent, done with his heyday but conscious of his national duty, makes a valiant effort to keep his only two sons on the farm. In English, he admonishes not only his sons but all young farmers to stay on the land and thereby support Osagyefo and the party. "Join the Young Farmers' Organization," he cries. The party and government will make life brighter and happier for low-income groups if they remain where they are. "And is it not a fatal fact that without farmers, a nation is always on the brink of famine and disaster?"

And, not unlike the fable of the city mouse and the country mouse, one son stays behind to work the farm, while the other chooses a life of adventure, romance, success in the big city. Sure enough, the city mouse returns to the farm with his city-bred spouse, and there's the rub. She,

68

knowing only the sophisticated life, is captivated by the "homespun virtues" of the brother who stayed home; *his* wife, having ventured no farther than a neighboring village, is wildly attracted by her brother-in-law's flashy clothes, hip city slang, and money.

Thus we have the enactment of a situation quite common in post-independence Ghana: kids forsaking tradition and family for education and the "new way" of life. Rural cooperatives and other government efforts to keep people down on the farm are encountering a hard core of resistance: urban living, even with all its slums, vice, and corruption, claims a growing number of the population every year.

Strange to say, despite the intent of this play, not one "big man" showed for the performance. Not the D.C., not the police commissioner in charge of the area, not the school principal, and not, for some strange reason, the Young Pioneer organizer. Only one other teacher besides myself attended, but I shouldn't have been so surprised: the "elite" were careful to avoid social contact with the masses, no matter what the nature of the event.

On my way home through the dark, quiet streets— quieter than usual tonight—I found myself peering into the faces of everyone I passed. Could I find the "true" Ghanaian—whatever he is—in this country of exchange citizens? Only recently I had met an old gentleman who had returned to Ghana after fifty years in Liberia, where he had gone to take advantage of American war dollars. He told me that thousands like him lived in that country as fishermen, traders, and professionals, only to return to their ancestral homes in their twilight years. And not only in Liberia, but all the countries between the Cameroons on the east and Dakar on the west boast a large number of Ghanaians, in some cases whole clans, the only link between them being centuries of tribal loyalty.

A Czech cartoon making fun of a pathetically miserable African lad appeared in the *Ghanaian Times* today and received a nasty scolding from that paper's editor. Had it been an American cartoon that had drawn such a degrading picture, however, the editors would have been far more indignant, and launched a scathing attack on the brute imperialist. "Czechoslovakia is Africa's friend, especially Ghana's, in the true spirit of socialist solidarity," and thus elicits only a dressing-down when she errs.

Perhaps the African knows instinctively that the barbs of the Easterner come more from ignorance than maliciousness. Having never occupied African territory, Czechs and Russians have had to depend totally on those stereotyped images handed down by the nineteenth-century missionary and explorer.

Had a good talk about the new GNTC competition with the most articulate Ghanaian I have met in Half Assini. He says that many people will continue to shop at Morkek's in spite of the low prices at the government store. Morkek is still a chief, and as such commands the unwavering loyalty of his clan: should he order his people to boycott *any* store, they would unquestioningly do so. It seems to me that modern governments in Africa would do well to gain the support of local clan leaders, not by force but by persuasion. The chief, as custodian of tribal tradition and law, exerts a powerful influence not only on his subjects who remain in the village but also on those who travel to distant shores. Indeed, it is the cohesiveness of the tribe and the attention paid to ritual that accounts for the Nzima teacher's using his own language, rather than the required English, in class; for the hellish battle one has to fight if he's been so wayward as to choose a marriage partner from a different tribe. Wherever the Ghanaian with strong tribal attachments resides, his

loyalty is always first to his tribe. Yes, Nkrumah and the CPP have their work cut out for them, even while they too honor such obligations.

Student friend Soboe seems to feel more at ease about discussing politics with me. Says that the border areas are on fire with people wanting to be part of Ghana. That the Ivory Coast police and army were moved in to extinguish the fire and were met with active resistance no doubt calmed the fears of the "rebels": regardless of whether or not it was politically expedient, Ghana was there to protect their interests. Probably why my Foreign Affairs friend had been installed in such a remote "outpost of civilization," as he put it.

To stretch the imagination further, it could well be that the new all-weather highway being built right down to the lagoon's edge, the new tourist "restaurant," the new and well-manned police border station, and the appointment of a new Deputy Commissioner for keeping law and order in such a sparsely populated area, are all attempts to make ready for a grand homecoming.

Soboe, like several others I've talked with, is convinced that an African politician need have no fear for his person or career as long as he can secure good *ju ju* protection from fetish priests and holy blessings from his chief. Hadn't both the Ivory Coast and the Ghana police searched him at the border, and hadn't they both failed to detect the secret letters he was carrying? Proof positive of his superior *ju ju* . . .

APRIL 6

As I complete this first of several notebook diaries, the rain is coming down in soft, gentle splashes. As many times before, I'll walk into town, and the people will stare, as they always do, at the crazy man strolling in the rain

71

without a coat, hat, or umbrella. And they'll also think to themselves, "rich" men don't walk, they ride.

APRIL 7

The boredom was terrifying. On an impulse, I made my way over to Esiama; but, aside from a track meet between area middle schools, nothing was going on there, either. Ended up in the hotel bar with Rocky and several of the local elite.

Two hours of steady drinking and nothing but promises . . . Threw in the towel about 10:00 after Rocky disappeared with a dame, not letting me know where or when he would return. Checked hotel for room, all beds wet from rain. Now seemed a good time to show Bobby Kennedy that I too could hike fifty miles, but two miles was more than enough to sober me up, and I settled down in a police check-point the size of a telephone booth, crumpled against the walls. Was this really necessary? I said to myself. I mean, what the hell was I proving? So it was a torture pit—and I was "roughing" it—and the Kennedys would be proud of me. Okay, move on, boy.

I straggled over to several nearby huts, looking for a room, a request that was met with snarling groans of resentment and hostility. The dirty bastards! If I had been a European they would have *begged* me to come in and spend the night. So, back to the pit and the mosquitoes and the worms and the deadly silence of an African bush night. Rocky finally came along and mercifully extricated me from the dark.

APRIL 8

Having spent a miserably boring day in Esiama yester-

72

day, I was delighted this morning when some of my students came by with a huge viper snake 4' 6½" long and having a mid-section the size of my thigh. With the help of Dick Maize, a visiting volunteer, we skinned it and tacked the skin down to dry in the sun. Ghana gin was to be the preservative, since there was no formaldehyde. The beast's heart pulsated with steady regularity even as we cleaned and scraped the skin, a performance that forced the kids to keep a respectable distance. The skin was later sent to two college chums as a wedding present.

APRIL 10

While in town yesterday, I noticed hordes of people rushing to the police station. I joined the pack and learned that a villager had been run over by a truck. People were wailing and jumping up and down—even the school matron and the District Chairman of the National Council of Ghana Women—but not so the police, who were taking this rare occurrence with more than a pinch of calm. They had removed the "murderer" to safer quarters: this mob rivaled, in its determination to have a piece of the villain's hide, a lynching detail in the South. I couldn't help thinking that if I, an outsider, had been the cause of his death, the police might not be able to assure my safety!

It wasn't easy to leave that spectacular display of tribal solidarity, but a letter from Boss Carter ordering me to Accra pulled my attention back to the here-and-now. Seven hours and a bloody ride later (the after-rain bugs were out in full force, splattering the windshield and literally blinding me), I was in his office and, within five minutes, in the doghouse: I was snooping around too much, asking too many questions, getting the other volunteers all worked up . . . Stick to the bush, boy . . .

73

Late in the evening Afro-American Volunteer Sims rushed into the hostel hollering for War, and, not finding him, poured out his grief to me. It seems that Fred, an Afro exile in the Worker's Brigade, beat his wife, a Ghanaian, then his mother-in-law when she tried to protect her daughter. Poor Fred, trying so hard to be African and not making it, never making it, for American Negroes are caught in just as much of a dilemma here as they are in America. "Oh, what has this white man done to us?" Sims says, his face crumpled in despair, and I sympathize with him, because I too am ashamed. Later, cringing on the roof till dawn, I find myself thinking about Odel, one of two Negro female volunteers here, who married an Indian and is already suing for divorce. And it is said she had even bleached her light brown skin to appear European . . .

For some time now I've held the notion that Peace Corps volunteers, being politically conservative—especially in the light of Ghana's socialist orientation—in effect do not support the government any more than those in the opposition camp. Grant, for example, a teacher turned geologist, is hypercritical of Ghana's aspirations, believes that she's trying to go too far too fast. "The British should have refused to turn over the $220 million in gold reserves at independence. Nkrumah has only squandered it on roads that lead to nowhere and an airline which sits collecting fungus on the runway. Man is naturally selfish and therefore inherently capitalistic, and, without individual incentive, will be lazy and unproductive"—a theory that goes a long way toward explaining (for *him*) why his Ghanaian assistants are lethargic and slothful. (And,

74

I was tempted to tell him, why he believes he could become rich if he remained in Ghana after his Peace Corps tour; and also why there is validity to the party's claim that volunteers are agents of American imperialism.) Why the hell isn't he, and all those like him, shipped back to the Ivy conservatism of the MIT-Harvard vineyard from which he came?

APRIL 18 – 25

It was summer vacation, and many months since Half Assini had enjoyed the company of so many "European" (white) visitors. For me this was a time to play host to volunteers from up country as they passed through on their way to and from the black French cities of Abijan and Dakar. (Peace Corps policy prohibits travel in Europe, so they chose the nearest thing to Paris and London.)

Almost to a man, they expressed unqualified admiration for these cultural oases: the cuisine was incomparable, the conversation scintillating, the manners flawless. Not one commented on the appalling squalor and poverty of the countryside through which they had to travel to reach the cities; nor on the almost complete domination of the economy by French nationals; nor on the glaring class and racial discrimination still heaped on the African masses by the French expatriates and their black lackeys, the new elite, referred to by certain African nationalists as "Black Frenchmen." Rushing like gazelles from the claws of a lion, these American and Canadian volunteers saw everything in these "outposts of French civilization" through rose-colored glasses.

Only Ole Bos, who had once hitchhiked to Abijan—"roughing it," he said—put in a word about the fishing villages along the way: it was obvious to him that Western civilization hadn't reached that far. Will someone in

the audience please tell me what the hell is so desirable about "Western civilization" that makes one feel sorry for those who don't have it? And if it is so damn desirable, why are these fisher folk frustrated whenever they reach out for it? But who was I to get so angry? Didn't I refuse to help one of my students prepare his "political treatise" the other day because I might be suspected of involvement in "local politics"? Here was a kid talking about "Africa for Africans," "removal of puppet governments," and the "destruction of the new class of French and African neo-colonial capitalist exploiters," and all I could offer was a suggestion that he ask someone at the Ideological Institute.

But there were certain light moments for me, even as I was barraged by one after another of these "dedicated, altruistic" souls. Such as the day I saw sweet little Gertrude, my forever-smiling pupil, sitting in the sand of her thatched-roof family compound thumbing through an old Sears, Roebuck catalogue given her as a gift by a relative returning from Liberia (that he would lug it through several countries tells much about the American presence), and, at the same time, literally beating a dress with a traditional rolling-pin-shaped "iron" made of wood. There might be no electricity in Half Assini, but Gertrude was going to catch up with where she thought the rest of the world was—at least the fashion world!

Or the afternoon I finally met old, rich Mr. Richardson, a Fanti who had earned the respect (but not the affection) of the Nzimas throughout his twenty-five-year residence in the area as local agent of the British-owned United Africa Company, a sprawling fixture found in almost every hamlet and town in former English colonies. I had first noticed him at a local dance, lounging, as most rich men do everywhere, in the "big men" section of the outdoor dance hall. He had seen me, too, but, as he ex-

plained on this day, he had been "afraid" to talk to me at the dance, "because of a conditioned reflex that all foreigners, black or white, are superior to us. You in America, especially, have a higher civilization, and before our independence we had always been in an inferior status."

And to think: I hadn't approached Mr. Richardson for precisely these reasons. He was a big man, cultured, dignified, and wealthy. Why should he waste time on a small-town teacher?

Half a century separates Gertrude and Mr. Richardson; yet they are alike in many respects. She too is "afraid" of foreigners and simply will not believe that a European or an American can be visited by the same ills and problems that beset Africans. More precisely, not that they *couldn't* experience these frustrations, but rather that they *shouldn't*. I remember vividly how upset she was when Arnold Zeitlin (author of *To the Peace Corps with Love*) and his wife, passing through on their way to Abijan, were trapped by a downpour and forced to spend the night on the porch of a local store. Not a little sarcastically, I had said, "White people shouldn't have to suffer that kind of indignity," and she had nodded vigorously in agreement.

That a fellow Ghanaian can be equally inconvenienced and get none of her sympathy is probably what accounts for the foreigners' appreciation of "African hospitality." Another example of the "colonial mentality" at work . . .

A not so light moment was had by all at the school when the secretary informed us that Ackah is in the clutches of a fetish-priest head shrinker, and will probably be there for some time, leaving the students to worry frantically about how they did on their exams. One of the students facetiously suggested praying to Nkrumah for the principal's speedy recovery. (Story had it that, during the infancy of the Young Pioneer Organization, all

members were told to pray to God for bread, and when that failed, to pray to Nkrumah, whereupon the bread came tumbling down!)

Humor may well be "the sugar of life," but it seems to me that most everybody around here these days is "taking his black." The volunteers who are right now swarming through Half Assini have contributed more than their share to the popular distorted "truths" currently circulating among those opposed to the Osagyefo and his party. One had even been rash enough to spread the lie that Adamafio and Crabbe, two detained former ministers, had been secretly hanged five months ago, and that the Minister of Agriculture, Krobo Edusi, had no intention of returning to Ghana when his trade mission to Japan was complete: incriminating statements made by some of those now detained made his own detention a certainty. What a fool he must have felt when Edusi *did* return from Japan and was *not* detained, and the two former ministers showed up—quite alive—for the proceedings of the public "treason trials."

Then, too, this was a period in which I learned how ineffectual had been a survey I set up for determining the extent of the volunteers' commitment in their schools and communities. My questions went unanswered mainly because they were afraid of incriminating themselves in some "subtle plot that had to be devious and detrimental to the Corps." A second effort—to compare certain African educational systems with those of Europe—also ended in failure: few African embassies bothered to respond, and those that did sent only tourist information.

Perhaps the most discouraging experience I had during this time was to read five short stories (all published in pre-independence Gold Coast) written by Blay, Deputy Minister of Education, and discern not one expression,

implied or stated, of nationalist sentiment. Instead, this ardent socialist cites his own position and wealth as goals worthy of achieving, so that the youth of this great country may also "enjoy the attention of beautiful women" and live in luxury homes. God help this nation's future if men like this determine it!

Yet, strangely, it was smack in the middle of this hectic, confusing, frustrating week that I was able to put some valuable pieces together in my own mind. I now knew that I wanted to stay on in Ghana after my work was done, whether it was to work a coconut farm or enroll in the university's African Studies program.

APRIL 2 6

On the return trip from a village a few miles away today, I was pleasantly surprised at the sight of a fertility doll strapped to a middle-aged woman's back. This was the first time I had seen the doll used as something other than a museum piece. A miniature one-sided replica of the female figure, with very pointed, youthful breasts, it is carried in the manner of a child on the backs of women wanting but unable to bear children, either because they are barren or past the menopause. Interestingly enough, the nose of this particular one was Aryan in shape, but—in true African style—charms and other magical ornaments adorned its neck and arms.

The *Daily Graphic* still carries "Europeans Only Need Apply" ads, but no word on Lenin's ninety-third birthday, an event that warranted a double column in the *Ghanian Times*.

Tried to reach Accra in time see the Corps high lord Sargent Shriver, but just missed him. From what I hear, the office was in turmoil, with everyone running hither and thither, trying to find a cage for his monkey in time

79

for it to be placed on his plane for shipment to Washington.

APRIL 28

Ole Bos just returned from his big game hunt in sparse northern Ghana with the White Fathers, an order of Catholic missionary priests. He didn't bag any game, but, to hear him tell it, Papa Hemingway never had it so good!

MAY 1

Boss Carter let me in on a secret: One of the new PCV's was sent to a bush school and was so frightened after spending one night there alone that he is demanding a transfer. They'll give it to him, too, damn them . . .

MAY 4

For the first time in months I braved the hazards of our superhighway and drove 150 miles to Takoradi for foodstuffs in our new jeep. It shook, sputtered, and rocked and rolled all the way. Six months of this and she'll be out of commission: as it is, the speedometer is already on the blink! Maybe our Accra staff would be less apt to complain about the comparative high cost of maintaining a vehicle out here if they were brave enough to try our road sometime. Once would do it.

Newspapers and books—what would I do without them? And Paul Lawrence Dunbar to ease this aching loneliness?

> A crust of bread and a corner to sleep in
> A minute to smile and an hour to weep in
> A pine of joy to a peck of trouble

And never a laugh but the moans come double
And that is Life.

Charlotte must have sensed my need, for she unexpectedly dropped by tonight, and engaged me in a little welcome sex play. But when she had gone and I was once more alone, that deep-down ache started in again, compelling me to down vast portions of corn liquor and stumble drunkenly through more of Dunbar until dawn began to sneak in over the horizon.

MAY 5

Ocran has been badgering me for months to give lectures on American Youth to the various village branches under his supervision. Today I finally agreed, knowing that Peace Corps Accra will have a fit if they find out.

We went to several middle schools in the district to arrange an itinerary, and found the principals quite receptive to the idea, though many of them had grave doubts about the Young Pioneer outfit. This was my first time in Beyin, capital of western Nzima, and I was eager to see the omanhene's palace, a partially restored nineteenth-century colonial fort, but the chief was having his scheduled bath and couldn't be disturbed.

Ocran turned in a good public-relations performance with the teachers. Quietly persuasive, not forceful but definite, he asked only for cooperation and a chance to prove that the rumor-mongers were wrong about the Organization. Besides, the government had issued a new directive to the effect that *all* schoolchildren had to belong to one of the several wings of the Young Pioneers, so there was no longer any choice in the matter. The Boy and Girl Scouts were no longer acceptable substitutes. And he confided to me, once we were alone in the jeep, that the YP's would soon be the only legal youth organi-

zation in the country. Those teachers, village headmen, and parents who didn't get on the band wagon now had precious little time to do so if they cared at all about their livelihood.

MAY 8

I was given the miserable task of supervising yaws inoculation this morning, miserable because I couldn't stand the look of horror on most of the kids' faces. Many of them had never had an injection of *any* kind before, and this was a damn big needle! That this was how their government showed its concern for their welfare didn't seem to put them any more at ease, either.

Immediately after this grueling session, the bursar cornered me and explained that the principal has finally decided to close down the poultry farm I built for the school because it's losing money. Jesus, *that's* surprising . . . And all those teachers turning out every day, putting in hour after hour—to make it one swell disaster! Well, at least *they* had a chicken in every pot!

A bright spot: Bob and Donna, college chums in Chicago, sent packages containing cigarettes, gum, books, and copies of *Jet* and the *Chicago Sun Times.* Lucky I had a friend in the postmaster, who agreed to foot the bill for a share of the booty: the import duty was almost half the cost of the items!

Late in the day I was stopped on the street by a friend of the postmaster's who claimed to know "2,000 Smiths" in the area surrounding Cape Coast and would be glad to trace the descendants for me as he had done for other Afro-Americans. I told him we had enough Smiths as it is, without digging up more, but he didn't get the joke . . .

MAY 9

I was nervous as hell: the time for my first lecture on American youth had come, and I was still looking for a place to begin. Leaping in with my eyes closed, hoping not to offend Ocran or the audience through ignorance or an oversight, I began by saying something about "collective responsibility" and went on from there to the individual's obligations within the socialist political ethic. Heavy stuff, and I hadn't anticipated the large number of non-English-speaking primary students on hand. So, with a translator at my elbow giving me at least verbal support, I bumbled along, wondering if I was reaching them at all. At the next village, however, I came into my own: the kids were really with it, and when I was done, even Ocran stood up and applauded.

MAY 11

Today, Axim. Tomorrow—the world . . . Was *I* riding high. The audience here was much larger than the others, and peppered with several party officials, some of whom congratulated me effusively when I left the platform. Wish certain volunteers had been as enthusiastic! But they were bothered by my detailed description of race relations in the States, which seemed to them a trifle *too* explicit for comfort. After all, I wasn't there to stir up anti-American feelings, was I? . . .

MAY 14

My final speech was given today in Beyin at the oldest Roman Catholic middle school in the area, Ocran's alma mater, and, despite a freakish downpour that caught everyone unaware, the room was packed to overflowing. Even the District Commissioner poked his usually un-

concerned face in near the finish and gave me his blessings. But it was Ocran who seemed happiest of all—so happy, in fact, that he offered me a regular column in the Regional Newsletter. While I hated turning it down, I hated even more the thought of being shipped out by an irate Corps.

So, somewhat dejectedly, I returned to the killing routine of classroom teaching. My first-year biology students saved the day by indulging in one of their favorite pastimes: asking excruciatingly explicit questions about reproduction. Only this time they suggested I take a girl student, strip her down in class, and "explain her parts," that they might better understand.

The poor girls scrunched way down in their seats, not daring to look me in the face for fear that I'd do it (for the sake of science)! These kids also treated me to a discussion on the superiority of cat meat over rat meat (and the party paper had recently carried the headline, "Americans Eat Cats and Dogs": what they *forgot* to mention was that these animals were eaten as part of a survival course).

M A Y 1 6

I'm learning to appreciate even a cup of that scarce commodity, water—while my kids are learning to appreciate another, just acquired by the school—a lawnmower. If my memory serves me, this is the first modern lawnmower I've seen in Ghana.

Took a refreshing bath at the beach (salt water's better than no water) and spent the rest of the afternoon reading the papers on my veranda and watching my small neighbor at play—a little brown baby wearing only a charm band around her stomach. Will it really protect her, I think, as I scan the headlines: "U.S. Race Riots Move to Maryland," "African Students Beaten Up in Czech"? . . .

MAY 17

Wish I could work a little *ju ju* myself . . . Ackah's at it
again—this time summarily dismissed nearly half the
student body (eighty-four of approximately 180) and told
them to stay home till they coughed up money for the
term fees. Obviously he doesn't give a damn about boost-
ing the enrollment, or else he would have stuck to the "in-
stallment plan" initiated by his predecessor.

MAY 19

This must be a tangerine month: the town market place
is overflowing with them. One month it's bananas, the
next it's oranges. Like the water in this place, when there
isn't any, there just isn't any, and when it rains, it pours.
A flock of hawks are circling overhead, swooping in and
out of the dark, heavy clouds. Ghana must be divided into
scavenger districts, for in Berekum and points east, vultures abound and hawks are scarce. No vultures around
Half Assini. Like the vegetation, the presence of scaven-
gers changes from east to west.

MAY 26

There seems to be no end to what the United States will
do in the name of foreign policy. Only today a self-exiled
Afro-American artist (obviously one who had beat a hasty
path from his front door, and couldn't care less about
what he left behind) told me of the repeated overtures
made to him by the U.S. ambassador: wouldn't he like to
project one giant, sparkling image of his own country on
canvas? See? he said with much sarcasm, his talent
was actually in demand here. Back home no one knew he
existed, but now, suddenly, he's recognized. Well, he has
no intention of being used as a political football, even if it
means anonymity again. Not that he lacks political con-

85

viction: on the contrary, he is, like most black exiles here, vigorously pro-Nkrumah, but he doesn't see why his reputation as an artist should depend on that fact.

MAY 2 7

Wonder if Dick Darman and his wife intend to live in the States (she's a Ghanaian). Most of their friends from the home of the brave and the land of the free are trying to convince them to stay here, but Mrs. Darman (who says she's never even dated an African) is anxious to leave. This despite the fact that her husband's parents heartily disapprove of their marriage. Boy, if she thinks they're an exception, is *she* in for a surprise!

As for *my* love life . . . the mother of one of my students (Josephine) called me to her family compound today and, through an interpreter, asked me to marry her daughter. Why not? I was an eligible bachelor, and Alabama wasn't going to raise an eyebrow at *us* (we'd be "sticking to our own"). Well, aside from the fact that I'm not all that eligible, Josephine isn't exactly my cup of tea.

MAY 2 8

Up to now, whatever I knew about "traditional" or "African" medicine had been gleaned mostly from the students and a few scattered references to Ackah's well-advertised "trips." But today I got it first hand when Blay took me to a village a few miles away to visit an uncle who is not only the village headman but also a prominent *ju ju* specialist. The layout of the rooms at his compound made me smile: a good old-fashioned U.S. psychoanalyst would have approved of the doors leading this way and that to separate rooms where the patients could wait—and be spared a run-in with a neighbor, perhaps.

86

But there any resemblance between this office and one on Fifth Avenue stopped. In the center of a huge court-yard was a sand box, looking deceptively like a child's plaything, but in reality a slaughter box for sacrificial sheep. I bent down to examine it, and just as I was straightening up, who should I see peering out of one of that maze of doors but Ackah! Blay, looking in the direction of my gaze, suddenly took me by the elbow and tried to steer me away. No doubt he didn't want me to know Ackah was there. Indeed, Ackah himself was looking at us with a "Dammit, what's Smith going to think of me now?" expression.

And, though I hate to admit it, his presence there *did* shake me up a bit. The gulf between us seemed suddenly immense, and I wasn't sure I could bridge it. Had a strange, uneasy feeling—the same as when Ole Bos's houseboy, John, told me of a village near Axim where humans are still secretly sacrificed, and their blood and heart offered to appease the gods. The Ewes, a group in eastern Ghana, are particularly noted for this practice, and their name still strikes fear in the hearts of their more "civilized" brothers.

MAY 29

Bursar says the new teacher from Ceylon is starting at 126 pounds a month—74 pounds more than a beginning Ghanaian graduate or a volunteer receives. What the hell—are *they* prejudiced, too?

MAY 30

While at Blay's office today, I noticed several laborers chopping up what looked like a pig. When I asked Blay if he thought they'd sell me a shoulder (meat being so

hard to come by in Ghana), he mumbled something vague, but when I pressed him, he spoke up loud and clear: it wasn't a pig at all but a dog! Well, I could be a vegetarian a little longer . . .

According to a fellow at the Bureau of Ghana Languages, Akan is to be developed into a national language. He was quick to point out that it is not the government's intention to abolish or suppress the other fifty-odd languages and dialects. A Fanti would still speak Fanti, and an Nzima his own native tongue, but all would be able to *read* one indigenous language.

Ole Bos and I continue to have problems. This is the fourth time I've opened the door on him while he's writing a letter, and seen him rather sheepishly cover the paper with his arm. I was just about to ask him what the hell he was hiding, when we were called to a staff meeting: the government has come through on its promise to cut the five-year secondary school to four years, which means that incoming freshmen will graduate with those who are currently completing their first year. "There is no reason why Ghana should continue to follow the inherited British pattern. National development demands acceleration on a broad scope."

M A Y 3 1

In my third-year health class this morning, the kids surprised me by asking why I don't put my hand over my heart and say Ghana's national pledge at morning assemblies. Well, they clean their teeth with pieces of wood: did I ask them why they don't go out and buy toothbrushes simply because people in "advanced" countries use them?

88

JUNE 2

This is the first time I've really watched the school messenger lower the flag. No American would ever allow his flag to drag on the ground or be handled in such a rude and reckless manner. Even a Young Pioneer instructor in Accra commented recently on the respect shown by the American Embassy marines when folding theirs. I'll have to clue this kid in.

JUNE 5

Found myself infuriated by Ole Bos again. How the hell can he have dinner every night with that eagle-eyed colonialist priest and be able to sleep? He, who's always telling me to use my head instead of my mouth? Does he really think that one has nothing to do with the other? That you can share a sumptuous meal with a white supremacist and a few minutes later "turn on" for civil rights?

JUNE 7

On the way to Accra, I stopped at the New University College of Cape Coast and had a talk with the principal—a European—about a teaching position in the primary school. While he believed that I was qualified, he had to turn me down, as most of the pupils were European and their parents would object to a "black" teacher.

Why should I be surprised, when even the American community in this town, "citadel of Ghanaian progressivism," recently threw a party at which certain Foreign Service officers found a chance to really blast off at Nkrumah. "The U.S. should pull out lock, stock, and barrel and let this thing called a nation go to pot," they

89

unanimously thumped. Ironically, the party was hosted by an Afro-American couple.

And now the Mariners, possibly our most successful volunteers, must return home because Ann is pregnant. "The hazards are too great," says Peace Corps policy, apparently forgetting that the *director's* wife was permitted to have her baby here.

JUNE 9

No water again, not even in town this time. And the rains came . . . Water, water everywhere, but not a drop then for bathing, flushing the toilet. Back to the outhouse . . .

Reading an article on India in the May *National Geographic,* I was struck by the many ways in which that country resembles Ghana: the use of charms to ward off evil spirits; hawkers on every street corner; strikingly similar traditional dress; *neen* twigs as tooth brushes; self-help an important instrument of government policy . . .

The little girl Ole Bos ran down in the jeep in Takoradi is doing okay . . . His jitters "have done gone" . . .

JUNE 11

The Times had all kinds of goodies on the front page today: a large photograph of King and "fellow warriors," captioned "Kennedy Has Brought No Change—Luther King!"; a message from Harlem's Universal Negro Improvement Association, Marcus Garvey's old back-to-Africa outfit, praising Kwame for bringing freedom and prosperity to Ghana; a smaller item with the headline, "African Shot Dead by Verwoerd."

JUNE 12

Young Pioneer boss Ocran paid us a visit today—to perk

things up a bit: the dignitaries arrive any minute to officially open the town's new paved roads, and the school's got to give a good showing. At the assembly, he did a fair job of explaining the Young Pioneer aims, but his assistant failed dismally in attempting to answer the students' pointed questions. When asked why membership was compulsory, he replied, "I don't know. The order came from upstairs." And as to whether a student would be penalized for refusing to join, the assistant was so vague that preventive detention must have seemed an imminent possibility, despite Ocran's earlier assurance to the contrary. A third question—"Why do you say 'Nkrumah never dies'?"—so agitated the assistant that he blurted out: "Nkrumah and Nkrumahism are different, but I don't know the difference, and don't know who started those slogans," at which there was a wild burst of derisive laughter—even after Ocran went to some length to differentiate between Jesus and Nkrumah.

Had a long talk with Ocran after dinner, during which it became clear that he wanted *me* to give *him* an ideology. I loaned him my copy of Nkrumah's autobiography, suggesting that he concentrate particularly on the meaning of such slogans as "Nkrumah does no wrong," "Nkrumah is our Messiah," and "Nkrumah never dies." He was quick to reply: "No one seems to mind when people say the Queen of England does no wrong. Nkrumah represents the people, therefore he can do no wrong. Second, Nkrumah is *our* Messiah, our liberator. Third, Nkrumahism never dies, not the person Nkrumah." I told him he would have a tough job, especially after today's debacle, convincing the students: the churches were obviously holding their own.

Snow was probably right: Mao could do it because Christianity and all those other depressing concomitants of Western imperialism never penetrated beyond eastern China. And St. Clair Drake, too, in saying that Nkrumah

would lose in a showdown with the Church. But Lipset hit the nail on the head in *Political Man*: organizations must give legitimacy to the governing body. Here in Ghana, Christianity is a powerful organization.

JUNE 14

The sun had long since left the rim of cocoanut palms, and the moon had begun its rolling in and out of the chocolate overcast when I finally said, "Fuck this loneliness" and made my way over to Armah's. Last night we picked up his colleague the signal-corps corporal and stumbled our way to the Paradise Bar. Satchmo's huge likeness, glaring teeth and all, still stared out, rather mockingly, at the customers. For a moment, home didn't seem so far away. But the moment passed.

Armah was obviously in a rotten mood: we had just sat down when he suddenly leaped up and began to shout at the few teen-age couples on the dance floor. "What the hell are they doing in a bar!" he grumbled. And then we found out what was really bothering him: his wives were at it again, and they were driving him crazy. The poor guy ended up by asking me if I approved of polygamy, and even though I knew how much he needed my approval, all I could say was, "Brother, you take as many as you can handle; I'll settle for one right now because I am about to bust a gut in this loneliness."

His anger—at his wives, at himself, at me—would not be contained; it spread to American whites. "If any more of them try to pass to the Ivory Coast, they'll have trouble plenty." This obviously wasn't the moment to discuss the matter, but I was all too keenly reminded of one volunteer who had recently refused to declare his money at the border and who, had I not intervened, would very likely have been dumped in the lagoon—figuratively speaking, of course.

Was in a reflective mood today. Armah's doing: his indignation could not be ignored. Neither could one simple sentence in the back of *The Times*—Nkrumah's *Toward Colonial Freedom* "must be taught in all secondary schools, teacher-training colleges, and universities." I have yet to meet a Ghanaian teacher who has even *heard* of it. Who will teach in this country of paradox upon paradox, where a bamboo grass-roof village of no more than two hundred inhabitants, set right on the ocean's edge, has access to not one but *two* modern concrete bridges spanning a tiny stream? Divided into two sections, each insisting on its own bridge, the village is actually contemplating a third—for the center!

Even more astounding is the fact that Fantis predominate in this place—the very heart of Nzimaland—and they fish! I was to learn that pockets of these fisher folk can be found all along the west coast of Africa, but this morning, as I waited for a friend at the foot of one of these very bridges, I could only laugh at the insanity of it all. It was later in the afternoon, when I found Ocran wringing with sweat as he took his charges through their paces, that my humor turned to sympathy. In fact, so great was my identification with him that I suggested we simplify several of Nkrumah's speeches and distribute copies throughout the district. He was overjoyed and urged me to draw up tentative drafts right away.

One has to start somewhere, and Parliament seems unable to tackle the social problems that continue to retard Ghana's growth. Only today, for example, after bitter argument, most of it con, the Minister of Social Welfare and Community Development retreated and withdrew the Child Maintenance Bill, which would have made fathers of illegitimate children liable for their support.

I realized that, should I follow through on the writing project, my Peace Corps and Ghana days were numbered. Only tonight the *Evening News* described the Peace

Corps as a "subversive element." But I must take the chance: Africa is too dear.

JUNE 15

The campus is a beehive of activity. Party cars threading their way in and out, followed by a mobile movie van and a CPP sound truck blaring "follow me" type of high-life music, brass bands thump-thump-thumping, masses of children twisting in their wake, banners waving—"Committee of Refusal-Samuri. Greetings Osagyefo Dr. Kwame Nkrumah. Long Life and Prosperity." And of course a retinue of dignitaries, all of whom were invited to the President's beach house for refreshments after the ceremony. I trailed along, eager for my first glimpse of one of Nkrumah's "string of mansions," as they are maliciously described by certain volunteers. It was surprisingly modest in all respects—sparsely furnished and simply decorated.

While there, I managed to draw the Regional Commissioner aside and hint at my desire for "involvement." "Politics control everything in Ghana at this time," he said, "and you would be well advised to wait until the situation is stable, then study it carefully before making a final decision." Great. A party stalwart, said to be among Nkrumah's closest advisers, and he doesn't even have faith in the government of his own making. I might as well throw in the towel.

Also met a guy who introduced himself simply as "an American Negro," but Armah wasn't accepting that. Said he got the word that he was an intelligence agent and I should keep an eye on him when he slept at my place. Much later, at my place, he told me he was an official of the Agency for International Development, had been in Ghana since 1958, liked the place, but hoped to transfer to East Africa soon. He even showed me his credentials.

94

Nonetheless, I wasn't taking any chances: I hid my diary. The writing project would have to wait: there was too much suspiciousness in the air.

JUNE 16

Stopped in at Blay's tonight just as he and old man Richardson (from whom he rents two rooms) were discussing A-Kwesi, Blay's sub-boss. Blay thinks he does no work other than poking into other people's affairs, but, since he's District Party Chairman, owner Mussey is reluctant to fire him: government contracts, his most lucrative source of funds, would wither like a fish cut off from the sea.

We polished off a fifth of what Blay called "African bitters," a concoction of local wild-growing herbs and Ghana gin, and, growing expansive, Richardson began to reminisce about the "good old days."

His friend interrupted him almost immediately, however, declaring that he for one was glad to see the last of those bygone days, when a man had to do such ridiculous old-fashioned things as sacrifice a goat to the gods when his second daughter was born. The Bible said nothing about such nonsense (he was a properly God-fearing man), and those who still followed the practice were as out of tune with the times as they had been twenty years ago—a comment that greatly offended Mr. Richardson, who, with all his sophistication, still respected African custom in matters of importance. Blay was not to be distracted from his condemnation of what he called the "primitive behavior," however, and it was from him that I learned who Ackah's "fetish priest" is: my host's uncle! According to Blay, Ackah is beyond cure "because he can be cured only by confessing his wrongs, and that

95

he won't do." (Not if it means surrendering a portion of his salary to his relatives!)

JUNE 18

At 6:30 A.M. my young neighbor, one of my "money-catchers," came up and said he had a dream in which I left Half Assini and won several pounds in the National Lottery. Had to give him the sad news that neither had even a glimmer of truth. I've asked for a transfer that hasn't come through, and have spent 7 pounds on lottery tickets and won nothing. I myself dreamt that a big new factory was going up in Half Assini, and that isn't true, either.

For weeks now I've been turning a phrase round and round in my head, and am no closer to understanding it than I was when I began. The phrase is "African culture," and understanding what it means is made difficult by the fact that there are so many tribes, each with its own set of customs, making for a multitude of "African cultures." For it seems that "African" is often a synonym for Fanti or Nzima or Hausa—depending on who's calling the shots, of course. To hear Richardson and Blay, for instance, one would think only Fantis were the true representatives of African culture, the Nzimas being "uncivilized," "back-ward," "primitive." The medic from the clinic at Tikoba No. 1 (who nearly fainted at the sight of blood when I took an injured student to him) shares their contempt for the Nzimas, citing as proof of their ignorance the esteem in when they hold the *ju ju* man. "They'll die on his doorstep before they'll go to the hospital at Axim," he says. "True," says Richardson.

"And not only that," says Richardson, taking up the cudgel, "during the night they pile heaps of their bad *ju ju* around the edge of the bush—even baked babies!"

96

Blay, though Nzima by birth, listens to every word and punctuates every sentence with an affirmative nod of his head.

What complicates the matter is that Nzimas attribute these very traits to Fantis and other outsiders, *theirs* being the only African culture worth mentioning.

I suppose I thought if I could pin down that nebulous one-who-is-African, I would also know why he considers the Afro-American as distinct from him as the white American. And he must, because he refuses to acknowledge anything meaningful to him in the Afro-American's struggle. I remember the day I planted copies of the *Ghanaian Times* in strategic places around the school, hoping for some reaction to an article on the front page: "Two Mad Dogs and Their Black Victim," in Birmingham. Only one student noticed the headline, and when I asked him what he thought, he said, quite without passion, "Those people are bad." Even in town, the people I talked to either didn't see the article or else had no comment. Armah was the only one who was angered at the white oppression of his "black brothers"; Richardson, however, spoke for the others when he said there was nothing to be alarmed about. Everything will be okay because President Kennedy says so . . .

I had never been more depressed. The only way a people can understand the problems of others is to understand their own first, and Richardson and Blay were still incredibly naive.

JUNE 20

After plugging away, I finally got some response to that Birmingham piece from my second-year students— wanted to know why "those people treat Negroes like that," and wasn't there a governor to do something. On

the whole, though, they still showed a certain disinterest: *it* was happening over *there* to *them*. Just one kid seemed to sense a connection between this incident in Birmingham and certain others in his own country, though he might not have known what to put his finger on, for he asked quietly, "Why did the white man come to Africa?" A good question . . .

On my way out of the building, I noticed the messenger hauling in the flag, careful to keep it from touching the ground. Well, at least I had accomplished something . . .

JUNE 21

According to the *Times,* free textbooks for two million kids have arrived in the country. And Blay tells me that Ackah and his staff have disposed of ten of the eighteen fowl I left on the farm. I don't know . . . the two seem to go together. How're you gonna keep 'em down on the farm? . . .

JUNE 22

Time magazine has just been banned in Ethiopia. I suspect that more than a few other African countries will follow suit. Rumor has it that the *Time* correspondent in Ghana has resigned because of the editorial distortions his dispatches suffer.

The District Commissioner is still "upset" by my desire to leave, even though I repeated (a lie) that it was for purely professional reasons. He felt a lot better, though, when I pledged half my vacation allowance to his Town Development Committee . . .

JUNE 26

Third-year student Bossah collapsed in class. Fell un-

conscious to the concrete floor. Unseeing glassy stare. No obvious cause. The kids think he has a *ju ju* curse on him, because he's an eastern Nzima and had a fight with two western Nzima classmates this morning.

Today is pay day, and, for me, bill day. Had less than 20 out of 52 pounds when I was done. Mensah got 20 pounds, mostly for booze; Morkek 18, also for booze. Still owe 3 to the tailor and about 5 to the wharf storekeeper, again for booze. *122052*

Biology class still the kid's favorite. One boy finally got around to asking about that thick white liquid that comes from the penis. But this time the girls showed no signs of being disturbed when I told them, nor when Ekuful asked what happens when a man presses a woman's breast. He looked at me dubiously when I said I didn't know, it depended on the woman, and why didn't he ask one of the girls?

Had a few beers with Ocran and listened to him howl his disgust for the Voice of America's "Special English" programs. "Americans think they're so damn superior," he said. "Why do they think we Africans need *special* English?" (The truth of the matter is that most Africans, including himself, actually enjoy these programs, as is obvious from their frequent references to them.) He was surprised when I told him that the Voice of America was strictly for foreign consumption and not broadcast at home. "Then it must be only propaganda," was his cynical retort.

JUNE 29

This was a day to remember. Ocran and I traveled to Takoradi to attend a send-off party for Teeteh, his boss. Scheduled for 11:00 A.M., the blast finally got under way at 4:30 in the afternoon with the presentation of a Young

Pioneer leader pin inscribed "Service and Selflessness" to one Ed Smith. After which a Reverend Stephens made a short but highly articulate speech on religion and country, pelting the large gathering with such phrases as: "Serve God and you serve the nation"; "Obedience to the teachings of Osagyefo Dr. Nkrumah is compatible with obeying the strictures of Jesus and Mohammed"; "Deliverance from poverty, ignorance, and disease are common to Osagyefo and Christ."

Then it was Ocran's turn. Not to my surprise, but certainly to my concern, he repeated almost verbatim what I had said on the lecture tour. (He's becoming too dependent on me; I'd better step aside while I'm still ahead.) When he was finished and the applause had died down, he turned to me with a slightly sheepish look and urged me to say a few words. But even before I could graciously decline, someone else had already taken the floor. It was obvious that they had seized this occasion for a political rally: in just a few hours, practically everyone had said his piece, leaving only me and a few others (slightly drunk) to our private thoughts.

Stephens was by far the most sophisticated and skillful orator of them all, a master propagandist, using my presence there as a springboard from which he leaped into the black man's struggle in America. I was so grateful (and so amazed) that someone at last saw the parallels that I felt obliged to say *something*—albeit innocuous—and was glad I did.

Incidentally, at several well-timed, apparently planned, intervals, and especially during Teeteh's speech, one guest would rise to his feet and the others would join him in a party song. Reminded me of my old Baptist church days.

Only once during the long session was the response less than enthusiastic: when one of the speakers referred to

100

Teeteh as "Our messiah of the Young Pioneers in the western region." There is only *one* messiah in Ghana . . .

JUNE 30

Students can sometimes be as frustrating and obstinate as hell. After all my admonishments and remonstrations in health class about not putting objects in the ear, one boy came to me and said that the top of his ballpoint pen lay lodged in his ear. It is, and he is now playfully showing it to other students. I ordered him not to fool with it but to go to the clinic where it can be properly removed. I doubt if he will.

JULY 1

Republic Day. I had been told that, unlike Independence Day, this was a national holiday Half Assini would be out in full force to celebrate. Sure enough, by 8:00 A.M. (the first scheduled parade) the sports field was packed with spectators. But, in the manner of most events anywhere in Ghana, this one was postponed to 2:00 P.M., and actually got started at 4:00.

The Young Pioneers, waving brightly colored banners and looking for all the world like kids after the Pied Piper, took the lead. At their heels, straight and dignified, marched the National Council of Ghana Women, all in white—a symbol of purity. Mostly elderly women. (One wonders how the gap will be filled when they pass on.) And of course it wouldn't be a parade without a big brass band—only this one was quite small. In fact, the whole entourage, including the D.C. and a few school teachers, was astonishingly meager—about sixty-five people in all. Also strange—no party or national flags or other political symbols displayed. Just those white circles around the

kids' eyes, as for any kind of celebration.

Had dinner with the students in their dining hall: kenke, a boiled, mashed corn concoction, cassava and corn sauce, and, for the first time, unboiled, unfiltered water. Needn't have worried: the stuff went down and stayed down.

JULY 2

Finally got the message from the kids that one should greet, wave, shake hands, or handle food with the *right* hand. To do so with the left shows disrespect, because it is the hand men use when urinating. And all this time I've been using whatever hand was free!

The *Spark,* Ghana's "revolutionary" little tabloid, says "neo-colonialism is the ultimate stage of imperialism." Lenin must be turning over in his grave at the deviation from his "capitalism," especially since *Spark* was also the name of *his* party organ.

Voilá! My students are finally blasting away at American racism. Hard to believe that they're sincere, however, when they keep begging for my assistance in getting there . . . But maybe things in the States are getting better after all, what with the Pope's liberal fifteen-thousand-word encyclical, new Afro-Asian pressure, a new Afro-American militancy, and—yes, Mr. Richardson—the present administration being what it is. I must ask Ole Bos to see if he can nudge that priest into letting a copy of the encyclical go—if he has any. By the way, while we're on the subject of America, John asked me if it's true that all white women are virgins . . .

Four volunteers, including one shamefully homely-looking dame, are in from the Ivory Coast. One, a young greenie, was fingering the two copies of the *World Marxist Review* I had borrowed from the library, then shifted

his eyes to my Pioneer medal, and I'll lay my last buck that he runs over to Ole Bos and says that Smith is a Marxist-Nkrumahist.

J U L Y 3

Visitors out before dawn. Why were they so hot under the collar over the murder of William Moore (a former mental patient who was shot from ambush as he marched along a southern highway in protest of racial injustice)? Afro-Americans have been giving their lives for centuries, but let a white guy buck the system and get knocked off and suddenly everybody sees the light. Bullshit . . .

I'm trying some of the wooden sticks used by Ghanaians to clean their teeth. The kids made it sound easy: first bite the wood, then rub it over the teeth. But I'm discovering that my choppers aren't that strong: a few days of this and I'll scratch the enamel off.

J U L Y 4

Saw my first public beating at school. This time (apparently it was a customary method of discipline) the Brigadier's son got it. He, a Ga from Accra, had been caught fighting with a girl classmate, a Yoruba (I assume over some tribal matter). He didn't move a muscle or wince an eyelid when given his eight with the cane. The principal took advantage of the assembly to announce that certain third-year boys have been smoking pot, and while he has their names, he hasn't sufficient evidence to expel them. There was an audible sigh of relief.

Had a crazy moment of feeling like a kid in Alabama again. One of my students asked me if it's true that when rain falls and the sun is shining, a ghost is riding. I had been told that it was the *devil* riding. How close I felt to this kid, and yet . . . so far away.

103

In typing up an English exam for one of my colleagues, I was struck by the number of references to Booker T. Washington: "Which aspects of his life appeal to you most, and how have they influenced your own life?" "How did [his] work contribute to the recognition of the Negro in the United States?" When I later asked my colleague what he had in mind, he said he wanted his students to learn the value of individual effort. For the good of the individual or the good of society? I asked. But he hadn't got there yet . . .

Ocran has a very comprehensive program scheduled for Saturday's Young Pioneer meet: foot drill, gymnastic exercises, some games, and time out for "ideological training" and discussion. He asked me to speak on the "evils of capitalism" and was quite put out when I explained that the Corps was breathing down my neck these days, and I couldn't—this time—but I'd certainly be there to at least watch.

J U L Y 5

I don't think *Time* magazine has ever given so much coverage to civil rights before, and when *they* rake the dust from their eyes, surely the American people must be awakening from a long, long sleep. They seem to think Kennedy's "package of civil rights legislation" is doomed, though. Well, I don't think it makes a great deal of difference one way or the other. Negroes don't really give a damn about Congress any more: they're through sitting on the sidelines waiting for the "law" to help.

Ghana's former Minister of Foreign Affairs, now detained, was brought to open court today on a charge of fraud. It's noteworthy that he's not up for treason; nor, apparently, has any connection been drawn between the recent terrorist bombings and his alleged misappropriation

of funds. As with the detained former member of parliament, also being tried on grounds other than treason, the Attorney General dismissed his defense with a swipe of the tongue and went on to build a strong case for his involvement in treacherous activities.

The defense pleaded that Adjei had in fact mortgaged his personal property to carry on secret government business—something a foreign minister should never have to do—and thus was entitled to a little extra for his sacrifice. As to where he got that "little extra," Adjei claimed the god Zebus as his benefactor. Well, while this may sound like a whopper to the Western mind, it is highly conceivable to many a Ghanaian. (Remember the student who told me a certain *ju ju* man could double any amount of money I named?) Unfortunately for Adjei, the Attorney General came back with the remark that "money-doubling spirits do not exist in the Republic." Remember, these are the words of a pro-Nkrumah Nzima to a Ga; but how the devil did Adjei achieve such a position of confidence and trust in the first place, if tribal distinctions are of such importance?

When I put this question to my students later, they shocked me with their indignation—like I had no business even thinking about such things. In fact, one student was so rude, calling me a "meddler" and accusing me of using Ghana only as an escape from the police dogs of America, that I collared him without thinking.

He had shot an arrow, and it had found its mark. After all these months I thought I had earned their trust, but it was obvious that deep down they saw me not as one of them, with the same problems, but as simply an American, even though a black one, as different from them as Ole Bos.

Well, it's about time I faced facts: I am *not* one of them, and never can be. I think I've always known that, and

105

perhaps what I'm really struggling for is their recognition, not of a "lost brother," but of one who understands and wants to be understood in turn. The boy I hit—will they someday realize that I was hitting myself as well? Seeing in that dark brown face with the full lips all the self-hate and feelings of inferiority that have plagued *me* down through the years?

JULY 6

Left Half Assini at the crack of dawn in order to make it in time for Ocran's track meet in Bonyere. When I arrived, he was just leaving the Rest House, having decided that it wasn't to his taste to "sleep in the village with the people" after all. We went directly to the Roman Catholic school where the "ideological teachings" were scheduled to take place and where the D.C. was already, at 10:15, well into his speech. We entered the room just as he was clarifying the Osagyefo's central aims in establishing the Young Pioneers: "to help primary-age students become part of national life and, in so doing, to revive traditional culture," which the missionary had tried so hard to repress. On the blackboard behind him, apparently left over from the last class, was a quotation from Lincoln. I'll bet every kid in the place knew it by heart: Old Abe penetrates deep here.

All in all, about five hundred kids participated in the event, with another two hundred pre-schoolers watching from the sidelines. When I asked why they had been left out, Ocran said that many of their parents had something to hide and saw in the Young Pioneers nothing but a group of miniature spies and CID agents for the party. But Mrs. Gbedemah, wife of the self-exiled former minister, was right now drawing up a program for these kids, and there wasn't much their parents could do about it.

106

I left feeling strangely excited, as if I had been in on the "making of a country," seen the direction it was headed in on the face of its youth, and was eager to share my momentary euphoria. I stopped off at Armah's and was glad to find a couple of his pals there as well, but none of them was the slightest bit interested in my "revelation"; they were drinking "French-side" wine and passing juicy little pieces of gossip back and forth.

We soon came to Ole Bos's recent guest, who was obnoxious at the border barricade when told by Armah that he couldn't take photos without permission. He had taken several pictures of a naked child, and, when cornered by Armah, said that the child had asked him to. Whether or not that was actually the case, Armah suspected other, baser reasons, and, in veiled terms, accused the kid of trying to exploit the youth of Ghana. When he got a snotty reply he drew his arm back threateningly, whereupon the kid suddenly did an about-face and literally begged forgiveness.

JULY 7

John tells me that Ole Bos is threatening to fire him again, this time for using his "master's" lamp. This is the fourth time in a week that he's come to me with this complaint. Maybe Ole Bos is afraid the kid's been talking behind his back. Well, he has, but so far his "nefarious deeds" are still a secret—at least to me!

This afternoon some of the "gang" dropped by—the old sarge, who is being transferred; his replacement; Armah; the Clerk of Council; and one of my colleagues at the school. They pulled out a fifth of Ghana gin and, with a great flourish, proceeded to pour a libation to the gods—on my living-room floor! After every few drops, they stopped to invoke the blessings of the gods and an-

cestors for the old sarge, asking them to make sure he'd find as "good company" in his new post as he had found here. With a few drinks already under their belts, they were soon back to their favorite game—putting down everybody but themselves, and especially those Nzimas who were lately gaining influential positions in the party. ("The bombs have scared our President . . . He wants his 'friends' to stick close now" . . .)

It was into this den of drunken lions that young Kwame stepped, albeit gingerly, for he had a sore on his ankle, a gaping hole at least two inches in diameter and half as deep, and already exuding pus. I rummaged in my first-aid kit and cleaned my young friend's wound as best I could, mumbling angrily all the time: the whole thing could have been avoided if he had only worn his shoes; but, as he didn't have to tell me, shoes were a luxury to be worn only on "big days."

J U L Y   1 1

One of my students has just been expelled for putting two girls in the "family way." The poor lad was taken before the student body, where his crime was revealed and—unanimously approved by the principal and his staff, with the exception of one who abstained: me—his sentence announced. After which he was escorted by the head student to the dormitory and given "ten minutes flat" to pack and remove himself from the campus. His whole future is probably shot, since no other school is likely to overlook his sad record. So, out to the streets and certain delinquency.

J U L Y   1 2

Dome-shaped clouds hugging a point just above the horizon, and me and my little fox from Esiama wrapped in

each other's arms under the mosquito net, waiting for rain. These are the lovely nights . . .

John had a new one today: says he now knows the white man doesn't like Negroes, because all who come to Half Assini go to stay with Ole Bos. He didn't seem to appreciate it when I told him that Al, a Negro, also stayed with Ole Bos, and a white group from the Ivory Coast asked for *me* at the customs barricade. Probably wants to get revenge on Ole Bos for all those tongue-lashings he's been getting.

The principal gave quite a lengthy lecture on the Volta River Project today—and was visibly pleased by the equally long question-and-answer period that followed. Only at one point was everyone's patience strained: an Accra boy, obviously anti-party, asked whether the loans, since they had been negotiated by the CPP government, would be honored *when* (not *if*) Nkrumah's government fell. There was a sudden burst of yelling and fist-banging, quieted only when the principal said succinctly that contracts are contracts and must be honored. This student had obviously forgotten, or chose to disregard, the fact that Nkrumah had been given a mandate to rule by the *majority* of the citizenry, and that they and many others would be in no school had it not been for the new administration's keen interest in education! But such is the way of the world . . .

Allah-Mensah has just been accepted at the new University of Cape Coast. (I didn't even know he had applied.)

His enthusiasm must be great indeed if he tells the "seducer" of his wife about it!

JULY 16

Ole Bos showed me a letter from his brother, Assistant City Manager of Savannah, Georgia. I could have guessed its contents before reading it: "Negroes are breaking the law in demonstrations," "People wonder why children are used," "Private business cannot be forced to integrate," etc., etc. When I told him his brother is sadly out of touch with the times, he told me to get the hell out of his room. Wasn't prepared for my pity, I guess . . .

But Ole Bos's letter reminded me of one I had received from a "dead" aunt months ago, telling me that my father was alive and well. I don't know how the damn thing reached me: it was addressed to "Half Assini, Africa." At any rate, I felt like answering it now, telling her that as far as I'm concerned, my father's dead. Ghana had given me a certain amount of courage. I wasn't taking bullshit any more—no matter *where* I found it.

My right eyelid has been sore and quite painful the past two days. John tells me my whole face has gotten puffy—I don't look the way I did when I arrived. He says it's too much booze.

JULY 17

Awoke to find my eye shut tight with mucous. Hurt like hell. Screw John and his theories—it's probably a spider bite.

Our worthy auto mechanic tells me that a Methodist middle-school teacher was fined 15 pounds for beating a student. (He says his real crime was leaving bruise marks on the girl's body.)

Had a wholesome Ghanaian lunch with Ocran—a welcome change from canned food. He says that students at the Nkrumah Ideological Institute are being sent out into the villages to "live with, talk to, work with, and learn from the people," as the party promised some time ago.

JULY 19

One of my students paid me a visit today and made me feel like a clean old man! They were beginning to worry about me, he said. At first they thought I was simply being discreet, but then they decided I really didn't know what was going, so . . . he clued me in—on every bit of lechery he could remember and then some he had heard. Apparently several of the sweet, shy things I faced across the desk every morning had either had abortions or were right now seeking them, while as many of the boys, not content with knocking up their classmates, were going out on the town. He also, quite jovially, reminded me of the day a few months ago when the students went on strike. Contrary to what I might have been told by the staff, the kids were incensed because Ackah's girl-friend had fallen for one of the students, and he had threatened to expel him. I tried not to let my mouth hang open as he told me story after story, but I'm sure he must have gone away convinced that he had been right: this poor fool had to be set straight!

Another shocker later in the day—the students had refused their lunch in the dining hall for the second time: the *gari*—another kind of corn dish—was infested with insects. They all came to me asking for money to buy their lunch elsewhere, but I had to turn them down. I'm as broke as they are.

Browsing through "Personalities in Ghana" in the Ghana Yearbook, I came on some amusing facts about opposition leader Danquah: Kwame is his middle name; he lives on Nkrumah Avenue; his ex-wife is Mabel Dove, who now writes for Nkrumah's *Evening News*.

JULY 21

Ocran's son, Kingsley Mensah (named after a famous uncle), is supposed to be in Great Britain right now on a study tour, but he squirmed out of it for some reason, so Ocran's there instead. Before he left, he lent me his *Fundamentals of Marxism-Leninism*. I don't know if I'll finish all nine hundred pages, but I'm going to try. No longer content with second-hand answers, and I've had it with Christianity. There's got to be a better system of arranging society—a revolutionary one. Like the man says, "Any man who is not a radical in his twenties lacks a heart, while any man who remains a radical after thirty lacks a head." Perhaps the fire will lose its heat in time, but right now I feel like fanning the flames.

Young Kwame's sore is twice as large as it was when I dressed it. He stopped coming for treatment, and I didn't press him. It looks like a raw, wrung chicken neck. Armah, his cousin, has two in approximately the same place. Both continue to limp around and play. I now understand where those revolting and disfiguring scars found on so many adult Ghanaians originate.

Ole Bos has a new jeep, and I have a new bike: bought it from the Mariners for a song—"Pennies from Heaven." Kwame and Armah just about went out of their heads when they saw it. Will give it to them when I leave, not out of pity but because I love kids, and any time I can pro-

duce that beam of light, a beam denied me in childhood,
I will risk hunger to do it.

JULY 22

Took time out from *Fundamentals* to gulp down in one
sitting Nkrumah's *Africa Must Unite*. Yes, the West
would have much to lose from a Union of African States,
the USSR (and of course Africa) much to gain. How the
devil does he mean to convince the United States she has
nothing to worry about, her financial interests are safe?

One of my colleagues burst in on my class to show me
a "confidential" letter he had received from the Minister of Education. *Animal Farm* was "being used by certain unscrupulous teachers and pupils as a means for
drawing unwholesome comparisons which are aimed at
bringing the Government of Ghana into ridicule . . . The
Minister has therefore directed that the book should be
banned from all schools and colleges within the public
system of education. It should not be used in any Form
[class] as a textbook nor should it be placed in the school
or college library. Both teachers and pupils are forbidden
to bring copies of the book to their school or college compound."

If this is what they consider an example of freedom,
God help those who are still oppressed!

JULY 23

All sorts of interesting tidbits in the *Times* today: A
British racist who called a Ghanaian "nigger" got de-
portation orders from the court, while another Britisher,
who put "Expatriates Only" ads in the *Graphic,* was axed
by his own company. Also a front-page article on the es-
tablishment of a party branch at Winneba Secondary

113

School. First to my knowledge in any high school. The claim of four hundred members seems somewhat exaggerated, however; I don't even think the school has that many students. Us chickens referred to as spies for the "War Corps"—cute little distinction from this paper. Which reminds me: the district party secretary said he'd let me know in advance when the next party meeting would take place. Well, it's been two months and no word from him. Maybe he agrees with the *Times* and just *forgot* to tell me. The hell with him. Ocran says he'd never trust a party leader who didn't subscribe to the *Party Chronicle,* anyway.

J U L Y 2 4

One of the students—the very same who disrupted the lecture hall after the principal's Volta Project speech—just got booted for forging the principal's signature, and stealing another student's watch and a fee receipt. Ole Bos, running true to form, thought we were doing the lad a disservice by not turning him over to the police. Damn his ass, anyway. But I can't be too hard on him now: the guy's suffering from a touch of malaria.

J U L Y 2 6

Three-hour staff meeting. Big division over what to do with confiscated copies of *Animal Farm*: Ole Bos and PCV Rolfson in favor of returning the books to their owners at the end of the school year (he's up one in my book) ; Allah-Mensah vigorously for the principal's burning every copy. Everyone was shouting at everyone else, and I thought there was going to be a major free-for-all, with the books as weapons, but someone finally came up with the bright idea of turning them over to the D.C. and compensating the students.

As the meeting came to a close, the principal, drunk

with bliss at having us all together in one room and at the same time, took advantage of the last few minutes to warn us against "aiding students' immorality" by allow-them to use our bedrooms—a remark that fell on deaf ears, I suspect.

JULY 27

Happy birthday, Smith, you have survived another year. Any presents? Yes, two—both letters. One had been sent by me to the Chicago Peace Corps Service Organization some weeks ago and been returned. No such group in Chicago. Funny—and I had been to their office once. The other was equally mystifying, since it had no signature:

> Dear Eddie,
>
> I hope you will be able to untie your hands because your heart is certainly in the right place. I know you have the will power and the intelligence to do it.
>
>
> Sincerely,
> From a friend who is aware
> of your great potential
> for good
>

I ran all over town trying to trace the author through local typewriters. No luck, even though there were few enough typewriters to check. Had to be someone who knew me well—Armah, Ocran, the postmaster, any of my colleagues—and yet who felt that he couldn't really talk to me—Ole Bos. Yep, he confessed later, said he wanted to wish me well but he couldn't do so openly, our relationship being somewhat strained, to say the least. Well, what do you know? He *does* care . . .

JULY 28

The school's end-of-year ceremony—Speech Day—was a

swell affair. All the local elite were on hand, including an army colonel in civvies who always makes an appearance at these shindigs but is never introduced or given a crack at a speech. In fact, the only thing I know about him is that he built himself a luxury home with a private mosque just outside Half Assini in a village of bamboo huts. Obviously likes being a big frog! . . .

Also on the platform were the omanhenes of both eastern and western Nzima—a truly remarkable sight, since they've been feuding for years, each refusing to recognize the other's suzerainty over his respective area. The eastern chief was chairman of the function, while his western counterpart held the honor of being first speaker. Both unequivocally denounced Western imperialism and paid tribute to both the foreign and domestic policies initiated by Nkrumah's administration. They were followed by a student from the Ideological Institute, who was unforgiving in his assault on Assistant Secretary of State for Africa G. Mennen Williams and Bobby Kennedy, the former for denying "political maturity of African Negroes" in a speech at the Institute, Bobby for criticizing Ghana's socialist orientation. He further added that, contrary to the criticism leveled at his school by certain "misinformed agents," the faculty there truly represents Ghana's policy of nonalignment: political scientists and economists from the East, philosophers and historians from the West.

Hardly worth mentioning in the same breath, but interesting nonetheless, Africa seems to have her homosexual problems, too (if letters to Dolly—Africa's Ann Landers—in *Drum* mean anything) . Speeches today had me making all *kinds* of comparisons, I guess . . .

JULY 29

I am now in Accra with bandages on both legs, one eye.

116

and my right elbow. Yesterday, after Speech Day doings, I was giving four students a joy ride to the wharf when I missed a right-angle turn and the jeep did a couple of complete flips, landing upright. Despite a few cuts and bruises, the kids walked away unhurt, not even aware that they were in a profound state of shock. I felt like an ass . . .

The storekeeper at the wharf agreed to drive us as far as the Half Assini police station: the road was too bad for him to take the kids the twelve miles to the clinic.

I was charged with "careless driving" rather than the more serious "reckless driving" or "driving under the influence of alcohol." Being friends of mine, the cops gave me a break despite my strong objections. They didn't understand that better friends would have treated my case as they would a Ghanaian's.

JULY 30

The Peace Corps was not nearly as lenient about the accident: I was suspended from driving and shed of my Ghana driver's license. I find it strange that although I had on short pants, and they could clearly see the bandages on both legs, plus those elsewhere, neither the acting director nor the administrative officer inquired of my condition. But I suppose that's as it should be: the students were their first concern. Funny—and I remember the day the acting director arrived in Ghana and introduced his family to the PC Secretary, a Negro. His kids just stood gaping at her outstretched hand, but then they were fresh off the boat from Virginia, and one could hardly expect otherwise—even for the sake of show.

AUGUST 1

After pacing back and forth in front of the USSR show-

room in downtown Accra for several minutes, I finally decided to hell with what our embassy would think, I was going in! What a rude suprise I had when I took a good look at the scant goods on display: unbelievably cheap stuff. Scattered everywhere between volumes of Marx, Lenin, and Hegel were all sorts of gadgets, watches, binoculars, etc., hardly worth the effort that had been put into manufacturing them. Only the children's books looked well made—durable bindings, good paper, vivid illustratons.

AUGUST 2

Went over to the Bureau of African Affairs to enlist in the "Liberation Army" being recruited for service in Portugal's African territories. I had hoped to see the director—an Afro-American and thus one who would surely see why I wanted to join—but he was out and I got his assistant instead, who, shocked at my bold request, drew himself up into a pompous balloon and demanded a life history from me. His office needed the information, he said, to "find out who our friends and enemies are," and then, with even greater pomp: "We help all black people who need protection from whites." Little did *he* know that *I* knew it was all bullshit, but, at this point, I didn't really care what he did with the information. My hat was in the ring, and even the U.S. embassy couldn't change that fact.

The Executive Secretary proved to be just as exasperating, insulting my intelligence by reciting the history of Portugal's rule in Africa, who was leading the freedom movement, etc., etc., as if I had never read a newspaper. He wound up by telling me that no Ghanaian, let alone any foreign black, had yet volunteered. I sat bored and almost broken. But at least he promised that as soon as

one of his men had to go to Half Assini, he would pick
me up and bring me back to meet the director and possibly a Mr. Cabral, leader of the struggle in Portuguese
Guinea, who would be in Ghana for "consultations" next
week.

AUGUST 4

Whiling away some lonely, girl-empty hours at the Lido,
I happened to meet Jessie Jones, Negro American fighter
domiciled in Rome, who was beaten unmercifully by a
Ghanaian last night. He was terribly bitter, not only
about losing the fight to this "primitive opponent" but
about the treatment he had received from Ghanaians in
general. According to his Italian manager and certain
other Europeans he had talked with, girls were hanging
on every tree, just waiting to be plucked. But, he said
angrily, not by him, even in this country of the black
man, where the black man rules. Why, in Rome, dames
a dime a dozen were at the beck and call of the famous
Jessie Jones. Didn't his prestige *mean* anything here?
Apparently not, so he's had it. Catching the next plane
out.

I don't know why, but when he left I felt even lonelier.
Why should I waste another year out here? The real
struggle is elsewhere, closer to home—the seat of
Whitey's real power. The black man worldwide (yes,
even in Rome) is politically, socially, economically, and
culturally bankrupt. Finis. Ole Bos's world . . .

AUGUST 5

Now maybe those desk jockeys in Accra will laugh out
of the other side of their mouths! The administrative officer, his wife, and I were driving to Half Assini—he to

119

check on the medical condition of the accident victims and to verify the "authenticity" of my report—when the jeep hit a rut in the road and bogged down to the fenders. After a few minutes of some pretty earthy complaints, we got out, rolled up our pants (the men, that is), and tried to haul the damn thing out. Sank to our knees. Were finally saved by a couple of young fellows—but only after they had enjoyed a good long laugh!

AUGUST 7

And here's the latest news, folks: Ghana signs test-ban treaty . . . go ahead, laugh: a lot of the volunteers did when they heard about Liberia's signing. The point is that these people, even without the means for making atomic weapons, are demanding equality in its broadest sense. And isn't that what freedom and independence are all about?

. . . The *Graphic* reports that several PCV's helped stranded travelers on a river ferry. Yep, *Times* mentioned the incident but omitted reference to PCV assistance.

. . . The Upper Volta may have no industry, a high rate of illiteracy, and all the other ills that beset a truly backward state, but as of today her people will be able to hold their heads as high as their neighbors': they've been granted a television network!

. . . The Northern Regional Commissioner is quoted as saying: "In spite of the influence of Western civilization . . . Ghanaians have been able to maintain their rich and unique heritage." (And yet, when plans for the new hotel to be built in his region were submitted for his approval, he turned them down: too "traditional," not "modern" enough.)

Tired of peering at the clouds skipping over the deserted campus, and wishing I had never heard of the Peace Corps, I decided to spend the day and night with my bank-clerk friend in Esiama. He wanted to put me up in his spare "lovers' room" in an adjacent building; but, as it was already being used for that purpose, I found myself sandwiched in a 7 x 7 hole-in-the-wall in his "regular" house.

When I asked him about a check I had tried to cash at his bank some weeks ago, he said the Ghana Commercial Bank had to send it back to De Kalb, Illinois, to verify my account before releasing currency for it. God, if I had known the procedure I would have gone to the British-owned Bank of West Africa—despite my earlier vow to do business only with Ghanaian enterprises.

Was good to be out of the forest, anyway. Saw two incredibly lousy Hoot Gibson Westerns, which the Ghanaian audience loved (being just as big on heroes as we are). Even my friend, a high-school graduate, sat through them twice, remarking to me as we left that I was lucky to live in a "place like that." And I didn't have the heart to tell him there was no Santa Claus . . .

News round-up again: Volunteer Newell Flather honored for building his school's library into a going concern. Henceforth the plaque on the front door will read: "Newell Flather Library." *Graphic* calls him a "peace man."

. . . The Ho Urban Council sues the Pentecost "sect" over land illegally held. I always thought that land was easily obtainable, especially for the churches. But Ho is heavily Roman Catholic and might be attempting to push

121

minority sects out. Or maybe this is a government move to exert more control over religious organizations in general. It's about time.

. . . The Togolese delegation to the Dakar Conference, stopping in Accra on their way home, made loud noises about a centralized political government in Africa—having just signed a defense pact with France. So much for their real interest in African political unity!

While in town picking up the mail, I had a brief talk with the owner of the Paradise Bar, who is also a coconut farmer. He's very bitter about the government takeover of coconut purchases from private dealers. Says the British merchants who formerly handled the crop paid 3 pounds per bag, while now it's down to 2/10: somebody in Accra must be pocketing the difference. From now on, he would pay 60 pounds to transport his to Kumasi and sell to a British "undercover" agent.

AUGUST 14

The D.C. (to whom I offered money for his Town Development Committee and then, doubting his sincerity, withdrew my offer) is still urging me to "contribute to the educational and social reconstruction of this new socialist state." I wonder if he knows what "socialism" means? Only the other day he was lamenting the government's intrusion into traditionally private areas, and wishing out loud that he had gone into private business instead of joining the party, with its meager salaries. (He manages to run a cocoanut farm on the side, however.)

The Ideological Institute has just assigned research students to their own districts—apparently overlooking the possibility that the students will tailor their findings to the fit of local leaders. Tribalism is not yet a thing of the past—not by a long shot. Only today I heard the

old sarge complaining about being transferred from western Nzima, his traditional home, to Eweland: the telephone service in that area was "inept and inefficient." To the incoming sarge, a Ewe, it was not nearly as "inefficient" as some things he had seen *here*. And the fight was on . . .

I couldn't help thinking of Mr. Richardson, who, with all his sour remarks on this "no-good Nzimaland," has managed to reap a profitable quarter-century from it.

AUGUST 17

Still no word from the Bureau of African Affairs. Cabral was in town, as I learned from the papers, but when I hitched a ride to Accra and again demanded to see the director, I was told to come back Monday.

Still clinging to a string of hope, I asked to see Dr. Ham, Dr. DuBois's assistant, another Afro-American who might be able to point me in the right direction. He suggested that I either quit the Peace Corps immediately and throw in my lot with Ghana, or wait until my tour is complete and, in the meantime, establish contacts for future reference. He was most sympathetic, and sorry to be of so little help, but why didn't I try Julian Mayfield (Afro-American novelist)? He was known to be vitally interested in such matters.

On my way to Mayfield's, making a last-ditch effort, I stopped off at CPP headquarters. A complete waste of time: got the usual run-around. Boss Carter was right when he said, "They don't trust us," but it was of little comfort for me to realize this now . . .

AUGUST 24

Back in Half Assini. Beaten. Mayfield said there was no

123

hope at all. Whatever fire and enthusiasm I had when I left for Accra is completely banked. I no longer even have a desire to collect news articles or keep a diary. If Richardson can be here twenty-five years and still be considered an "outsider," what can I, an outsider from a totally different world, hope for in two years? That's right, "nothing," so it's back to the States and maybe "something."

AUGUST 26

Ahene is having financial problems at his store. His profits have fallen drastically since the government instituted rigid price control to stamp out profiteering. Several other small storekeepers in the same spot are giving up their businesses and looking for positions either with the government or with larger, more viable private firms. Of more than fifty small, privately run concerns scattered in and around Half Assini, it is likely that only the United Africa Company store can survive another two years. Even if the government didn't run these small firms—most of which are simply tables set up in someone's home—out of business, the giant foreign-controlled monopolies would. But the people are counting—and the government thus adds another group to a growing list of opponents.

AUGUST 28

A big day in Washington, D.C. If only the Bureau had knocked me down sooner, I'd be there right now. Carter, clever bastard that he is, arranged to take his business trip now, so he could be in on the march. Just before he left, I broke it to him gently—told him I was resigning from this turd hole. He merely nodded. Well, I guess he'd

124

just about had it with me and "my mission here!"

With only a short time left, I decided to sight-see in Takoradi—probably the last time. Buying two dozen eggs and bringing them back that 150 miles was like cuddling a day-old infant in one's arms while running an army obstacle course. The damn school truck had to stop every fifteen miles or so because of a "hot" coil, and the driver had to climb out, dip rags into pot holes of water, and wrap them around the coil to cool it—a procedure that took at least a half-hour every time.

When I finally got home, I found Blay waiting for me: a stranger was roaming around the campus—looking for me, he suspected. Probably an intelligence officer. But what the hell made him think he was looking for *me*? What crime have I committed?

When I asked Armah about it later, he said he didn't even know the guy was around—couldn't: he'd been out of action with a serious bout of yellow fever. When I told him I was leaving Half Assini, he seemed genuinely saddened, and only hoped he'd be well enough in time to give me a traditional send-off party.

My friend at the Institute (the same who had urged me to become a Ghanaian citizen) was the only one who seemed miffed at me for wanting to leave. Why couldn't I be content to quit the Corps, and not the country as well? Besides, how could I want to go back to America, anyway, when Negroes are treated so badly there? Well, I wasn't so sure they were treated much better here, and, ironically, at least I might be able to help them if I went home.

AUGUST 29

DuBois is dead. From New England to Ghana, from an advocate of democracy to a communist, from hope to de-

125

spair. It seems only fitting that he should die on the evening of the march on Washington, that on the day of his death, picketers were converged at the American embassy demanding in 1963 what he had said was ours in 1903. My one regret was that I had lost my last opportunity to talk to the old gent.

And here in Half Assini, where no one had even heard of DuBois, another funeral procession was under way: the deceased a young girl who once worked for our school and was dismissed because she allegedly incited the students to strike against the poor food. According to one of her relatives, she had been cursed with *ju ju* for her misdemeanor by another woman at the school. I was also told that her mother was asked to pour a libation to the gods for her daughter, and when she refused (out of fear of the "assassin's" *ju ju*), she too fell dead this afternoon. Both bodies were being taken to the local Roman Catholic Church—punished by pagan gods, redeemed and forgiven by a Christian one!

When the ceremony was over, and the crowd began to disperse, my attention was caught by the sudden appearance of a young girl with a cleanly shaven head. When I asked if it had something to do with puberty ritual, she laughed and explained that her head was shaven as part of her treatment for smallpox. When I looked doubtful, she pulled the top her dress down and revealed a lingering scar on her breast. Her face was as clear as a new babe's; in fact, her entire body was free of scars, with the exception of that one pockmark, if indeed her ailment was smallpox and not chicken or cow pox.

AUGUST 31

A few weeks ago I requested about a thousand books from the Alpha Phi Omega fraternity at Northwestern, and to-

day they finally arrived. After spending all afternoon and half the night sorting and listing them, I discovered, to my great disappointment, that only two hundred were suitable for high school kids: the rest were much too advanced. But they're better than no books. The principal was overjoyed, and so were my other colleagues, all of whom went immediately to the library and cleared the shelves of their dog-eared texts to make room for their new ones. Seems like I'm "in" again—even Allah-Mensah left smiling with an armful.

Speaking of Allah-Mensah, his wife's mother has threatened him with a *ju ju* fate for failing to honor a promise extracted by his in-laws on the day of his wedding: namely, to educate their daughter. Once they were married, the girl became his mistress and therefore—in Allah-Mensah's eyes, at any rate—hardly worth educating. His mother-in-law, however, saw things differently, and Allah-Mensah, responding to the seriousness of her threat, promised to send the girl to school as soon as it reopened.

SEPTEMBER 2

Holy fetish, somebody just returned an open pack of cigarettes via registered mail! It's addressed to the Customs Branch of the Ghana Police, mailed in Accra, and sent from the Comptroller of Customs and Excise. Why is it registered? *Ju ju?* No, no, I just remembered that I left a pack of open cigs at the Customs sarge's house a few days ago. So he's simply returning them to their rightful owner. God, what honesty!

My stomach's been bugging me for days—cramps, but not like anything I've ever had. And last night I noticed about fifty small bumps on my lower abdomen. John thinks they're bed-bug bites, but I sprayed my mattress and blanket and now there are even more of the damn

127

things—on my back and ass, too. Neck feels stiff, slight headache. *Now* John thinks it's malaria! Damn his diagnosis anyway . . .

After sleeping fitfully for a couple of hours, I dragged myself into town to forget the pain. Something was going on: a big brass band was marching down all the main streets, followed by a woman and an elder in a kente. I thought a new chief was being installed (traditionally the "incumbent" parades through his own village, showing that the elders approve of him, on his way to Beyin to seek the approval of the supreme chief, the omanhene). But this was no festive occasion: eleven people had died in the village in the past two weeks . . .

SEPTEMBER 3

Woke up with my neck in a vise and the left side of my body covered with a strange rash (the bumps had obviously banded together!). Ocran, back from England, stopped in for a chat and was horrified when he saw me. Said the band was still going strong in town, and everyone was praying to the gods for an end to the slaughter, and if I didn't want to be the twelfth victim of this "epidemic," I'd better get over to his mother's right away for treatment. I readily agreed—at this point I was willing to try anything.

The minute his mother saw me, a knowing expression crossed her face (I must really have looked like hell), and she ran to the kitchen, only to return a short while later with a pot in which red peppers (at my request, one pod instead of the usual four), leaves collected from the bush, and bark from a tree had been boiled. I was then told to go to the public john and give myself an enema, an order I pretended to carry out: if I was going to have to drink that brew, I might *really* need one later. But

when I returned, she merely rubbed some of the mixture over the rash and admonished me to go home and rest. Later, when I told Ocran that my grandmother used to collect herbs and administer treatment in much the same way as his mother, his face lit up with joy: he was afraid I thought she was a quack, and allowed her to treat me only to have something to tell my family and friends about back home. Hell, nothing in my first-aid kit worked, and I was damned if that lousy doctor in Axim could do better. Besides, I had nothing to lose but my chains . . .

SEPTEMBER 6

Three days have passed, and I'm still itching like hell. Rash seems to have spread, but at least the cramps are gone, and I can move my neck without pain. How much longer, oh God? . . .

Ocran stopped in to see how I was getting along. When I asked him how things were going with the YP's, he looked crestfallen: rumor had it that the National Organizer was involved in the bomb outrages. Ocran had moved that a vote of *no confidence* be passed and that a team led by the Regional Organizer deliver it to the "criminal" and demand his resignation, but the R.O. turned down his request: all scholarships assigned to the region would be withdrawn. So the bastard stays . . .

SEPTEMBER 9

Armah made good his promise and threw a beach party for me—a small, intimate affair, with more booze than people. I was really quite touched that they would treat me to the works—speeches and all—just as they would their "own."

On my way back from the beach, tripping less than

lightly on my toes, I ran into a horde of people at the cocoanut-collection office. A huge 1-1/2 ton truck loaded with cocoanuts had rammed into one of those hundred-year-old trees, pinning the driver and his buddy between them. The people had somehow managed to get them out, and now they were lying spread-eagle on the ground. Women took turns fanning them. A hell of a lot of good *that* did. They should have been on their way to the clinic, but, as is the rule in such cases, they were waiting for the police to come first. There they were, groaning with pain, and no one even dared give them first aid without a cop's okay.

It's probably just as well I'm leaving Half Assini on Wednesday: it's beginning to hurt to smile . . .

SEPTEMBER 1 6

I've been in Accra for a few days—as ordered, and against my will—helping to "orientate" the new PCV arrivals. They're a noticeably undynamic group compared with ours, and seem interested more in consolidating their own intimacy than in going out on the town.

But it wasn't a *total* waste of time: a Ghanaian friend took me girl-hopping—a new experience to me—in Accra, and I was amazed to discover that Ghana has a red-light district. Dark, dismal alleyways, and row upon row of 12 x 12 shacks with split bamboo walls, lamplight breaking the spaces between the shoots. In front of each, an immobile, quiet, statue-like figure of a woman. Old or young, they didn't utter a word as we passed. A strange, eerie sight, like an other-worldly painting I saw at the Chicago Art Institute some summers ago. Deathly. All transactions were done in absolute silence. A customer would walk down the rows, choose a dame, open the shack

door, and go in; the seller would pick up her stool, put it on her head, and follow him.

When I told my friend I wasn't interested, he merely shrugged his shoulders as if to say, "That's *your* problem," and took me to a neighborhood bar. It was here that I was introduced to a "bomb victim"—a young woman who, though badly hurt, was as vigorously pro-Nkrumah as she had been before the incident. She must have had great doctors, too, for there wasn't a scratch on her (at least that I could see).

SEPTEMBER 1 7

Finally got new assignment—Mpraeso—but it's only a stopover until Carter finds me a permanent post. The town sits perched atop Ghana's largest inhabited mountain, 2,500 feet above sea level. Had to drive almost straight up to get here!

I'll be living with the bursar. No running water in the house, no screens or fans either, but then I probably won't need a fan—it goes down to about 50 at night—and there shouldn't be any mosquitoes at this height. Actually, my room's pretty bare—practically no shelves for my books, and a minuscule closet. But at least it's a place to bed down, and it's cheap. Can save more if I eat Ghanaian food, too, but I won't compromise on the water. Must be boiled.

Am now lying on hastily set up bed staring at ceiling. Shock. A giant mosquito playing around. Damn it! And the ceiling is too high to attach a net.

SEPTEMBER 1 8

I'm glad I'm living with a Ghanaian. The other PCV here,

131

white like Ole Bos but less obnoxious, and I probably would have come to a parting of the ways soon enough. But I'm not so sure I like this altitude—felt quite dizzy in class, bumped into several objects. They tell me it will pass. Wish my rash would!

SEPTEMBER 19

Well, I had my first good breakfast in Ghana. The bursar's sister fixed us some hot oatmeal, coffee, and a nicely fried egg on toast. Couldn't ask for better anywhere.

Learned in town that the large white cross hanging over the face of our cliff was put up by Catholic missionaries. Adventurous chaps. . . .

SEPTEMBER 21

Sipping brandy alone (haven't made any friends yet) in "celebration" of Founder's Day, and watching the world pass by from my garret window: Young Pioneer squad, Trade Union Congress groups, all waving signs and banners—"Africa Must Unite," "The Imperialists Won't Stop Until They Quit Africa," "Long Live Osagyefo." Now some notable Moslem leaders, the principal and his staff, all wearing Young Pioneer scarves. This makes Half Assini's parades look sick.

SEPTEMBER 25

A Negro out of Peace Corps/Washington stopped in today to take photos and get a rundown on what Negro volunteers think of their assignments, students, etc. I must say his visit did my cynical old soul some good—at least *somebody* back home was interested in the Afro-

American's opinion, and was even letting *him* give it . . .
When he learned I was from Birmingham he rummaged
in his suitcase and came up with a recent issue of *Time*
in which there was a big spread on Alabama schools.
Jesus, how times had changed. There was a picture of a
school about a mile from where I grew up, but in those
days I walked ten miles to and from an all-Negro school
—and to think I never realized the insanity of it then.

SEPTEMBER 2 6

Finally (now that my school duties are done here) got
around to a book I've been meaning to read for years—
Gunther's *Inside Russia*. Interesting to note certain
similarities between that country and this: "One reason
why the bureaucracy is so cumbersome is that . . . there
are two bosses in every town, the party secretary and the
chairman of the local soviet." In Ghana the set-up seems
to be pretty much the same, with the District Commissioner assuming the role of the local Soviet chairman.
". . . One recent proposal is to the effect that high
school students, *before* they enter the University, shall
be obliged to spend two years at work on some job." In
accordance with a new policy proposed by Nkrumah a
few months ago, middle- and secondary-school students
are expected to work summers; university students the
first six months after graduation.

SEPTEMBER 2 7

The bursar finally got up enough courage to ask me if I
liked girls: he hadn't seen me with one since I arrived,
and was obviously concerned. And, while I resented the
question, I also realized that he hadn't asked anything
that hadn't been asked many times before—by my rela-

tives, by my fraternity brothers at Northern Illinois, and even by friends in Half Assini.

What I couldn't tell him or the others was that for many painful years I ran hither and thither looking for that good life everyone else seemed to be having. Only I discovered what was good for them was not so good for me. While I loved the company of people, I couldn't, no matter how I tried, make small talk, couldn't dance, couldn't "mix" well, in other words. And I still don't mix well, with the difference that now I don't mind that fact. It's really too bad that others do, because actually I'm quite happy to sit with a group, enjoy their company, and at the same time enjoy my own thoughts. For instance, last night it was good being with the bursar and his brothers. They were conversing in their own language and having a ball. I was too, but in another way: the music and the booze were fine, and I was savoring little bits of Gunther, reliving Half Assini days, fitting myself into the stream of a struggle far from this cozy room (a stream, incidentally, that would carry me deep into the heart of Ashantiland—Berekum).

SEPTEMBER 2 8

I would be spending the next three days in Accra—looking for a nail clippers, among other things! Sounds crazy, I know, but one doesn't appreciate the importance of such a small thing until it can't be found.

A second search took me to Young Pioneer headquarters: I hoped to see Teeteh and ask his help in getting me attached to his Youth Council, but I was told he had left only last night for the People's Republic of China. He certainly gets around: last time it was the USSR, at the invitation of *their* Young Pioneers . . .

It had been quite a while since I'd seen any volunteers,

so I decided to have dinner in the hostel dining room. The first thing they asked was if I had seen the bulletin board —a petition to Congress to pass the Civil Rights Bill. Jesus, the history of the Negro in America seems to be one of petitions. Well, this was one time I wasn't going to put my John Doe to that history. Let others make the symbolic gestures—like these volunteers, for instance, who were so damned contemptuous of the Ghanaian's gestures.

SEPTEMBER 30

Was taken by a Ga friend to a name-giving ceremony for a new baby in that area of the city where his people originated, and, for the first time in Ghana, was met with hostility when introduced: nobody extended a hand or said a word in greeting; they just stared stonily, as if I was putting my nose into "sacred" affairs that are not the concern of strangers. After a while even my friend felt the rejection and took me for a long walk through town. We soon parted company, he to have a few drinks, I to meet another friend—a Negro embassy official. He told me of his bitter disappointment with the American community here, how inbred it is, and how he, being married to a white woman, is merely tolerated. We also discussed a letter in the August 24 *Christian Science Monitor* from a depraved ex-serviceman and were drunkenly together in the belief that most American whites felt pretty much the same way. This guy happened to be from Portland, Oregon:

> I believe an examination of the records of the Air Force and of the reports of General Mark Clark will illustrate that the percentage of abortive flights in the Air Force when the pilots were Negroes was many times higher than in the case of white pilots . . .

135

From the experience of an officer whom I know personally, who was stationed in the South Pacific during World War II and in command of Negro troops, these troops were utterly useless at night. They were so superstitious and frightened that they completely refused to leave their quarters during darkness.

Now there is no question but what Negroes are entitled to their right to advance, but I do not believe that articles and speeches which contend that Negroes are equal at this time, as to education, moral stability, moral courage, knowledge, and judgment, to white men are realistic.

BEREKUM

BEREKUM, where I spent most of the second year, was an altogether different proposition. Located about thirty-five miles east of the Ivory Coast border, and hugging the northern fringe of the rain forest some one hundred miles north of Half Assini, this city, though small—around eight thousand people—has all the trappings of a thriving commercial center. The Brongs and Ahafos who live here are nearly self-sufficient, reaping sizable profits from their many cocoa plantations and vegetable farms, which in turn contribute significantly to the nation's economy. Compared with the Nzimas, the Brongs and Ahafos, being closer relatives of the powerful Ashanti, are more advanced culturally and technologically. They are known over the world particularly for their intricately carved wooden statues, their woven kente cloth, and, to a lesser extent, their gold weights and ornaments.

Berekum itself is controlled by an omanhene, whose immense concrete house faces a large parade ground in the center of town. All important traditional and party functions are conducted here, and the omanhene, as expected, attends every one he can; but I was told practically on arrival that he's vigorously anti-party and puts on a show of loyalty only to avoid the dreaded fate that befalls so many outspoken Ghanaian chiefs: destoolment.

All of the main streets in Berekum are paved; by

Ghanaian standards the highway to Kumasi is a major accomplishment, and I heartily agree, remembering the fair-weather trail leading into and out of Half Assini. All of the elementary schools in town and most of those in outlying villages are of concrete-block construction with tin roofs, but, like those in Half Assini, these schools have absolutely no science equipment or libraries. The one hospital in town is small but extremely well staffed and equipped, and is run by an order of Roman Catholic nuns, most of whom are Americans with long years of missionary service in Africa. Their nurses' training schools enjoy unusual prestige in a country so dominated by "anti-American" slogans and ideology. (I for one was greatly admiring of it: at last my biology classes had a lab!)

Government Training College specializes in the preparation of teachers for the nation's rapidly expanding primary and middle schools. It was one of the first teacher-training institutions set up by the CPP government when the British gave the reins to Nkrumah and his colleagues. Much care and money had gone into the planning and construction of the school, and it shows: modern ranch-style bungalows, some of which have hot-water tanks, spacious well-packed sand-gravel streets, a meticulously tended landscape, a broad library, a small but pleasing guest house that was intended for visiting lecturers but is often pre-empted by visiting party functionaries, and a carefully selected staff. Few schools can claim such high standards, and, as a result, the waiting line for teachers as well as students was long indeed.

Sunyani, the area headquarters for the government and party, is a buzzing town some ten miles to the east. Only recently replacing Berekum as the regional center of activity, it has a small government hospital, a new secondary school, various government offices, and a very

modern "rest house" stocked adequately with assorted imported booze and pretty African girls. This is the one place where Russians, Africans, English, Americans, and even an occasional Chinese can be found indulging in a common luxury—getting away from it all.

But just a few weeks in Berekum and any desire I might have had to get out and "meet the people" was all but gone in the killing boredom of the long lonely nights. Even with all its charms, Berekum was still bush country, and I didn't fight to get out of Half Assini in order to get another bush—no matter how carefully pruned. The people were more than congenial, the school excellent, but I now wanted to get to Accra with a passion. The academic life had lost its allure for me: damn the long-range goals; let me get to the nitty gritty. March, fight, spy, shoot, die . . . Go to Angola, Mozambique, Portuguese Guinea . . . Get back home and march on Washington, shoot some Crackers . . .

OCTOBER 1

This is a Peace Corps first, no volunteer has ever before taught in a teacher-training institution in Ghana. I better watch it or I may be the last . . .

My first day and I already had a few words with the principal! He's informed me that I'll be teaching science, not education, which I prefer. But a long, leisurely walk around this beautiful campus and I forgot to be unhappy.

God, what a change from Half Assini! For one thing, the school has a teachers' lounge (which is exactly what it says it is), replete with squshy sofas, armchairs, and a radio that is seldom not in use. For another, there's a water cooler in the main hall, a double tennis court, a *poultry* farm . . . One distressing thing, though: each bungalow has its own water filters, and that's great, but

I'd had enough mosquitoes to last a lifetime, and I wasn't crazy about the idea of living in a net cocoon again.

OCTOBER 2

Berekum has just about everything you could possibly need—everything, that is, except a nail clippers! And the sight of a movie house drove this bush man out of his mind. I saw four movies in one sitting—really dug the last, from Prague, "African Friendship." Shots of black guys and white girls kissing, probably a staged intimacy, but effective nonetheless.

OCTOBER 3

Spark is blasting neo-colonialism again and accusing all African countries except Ghana, Guinea, Mali, and the U.A.R. of failing in their struggle for "complete independence from foreign rule," and of only half realizing the socialist way. From what the principal in Mpraeso told me, Tito wasn't even this kind: riveting his attention on some small private business he chanced to notice while touring Ghana, he reportedly scoffed, "And you say you are building socialism?" (Interestingly, almost simultaneous with his tour, the term "African socialism" was coined.)

Who in the hell does Tito think he is, criticizing the Ghanaian brand of socialism, when 90 per cent of all land in Yugoslavia is privately owned, and small private shops and stores flourish (*New Republic* figures)?

OCTOBER 4

The principal threw a blast at his place tonight, and

everybody tried to make me "feel at home" by shoving dames at me from all directions. Didn't want to hurt their feelings, but made it clear I preferred making my own arrangements with the chicks.

One guest, an English teacher and one of the school's four college graduates, gained my immediate interest when he brought up the race riots in Alabama to illustrate what was obviously uppermost in his mind: the barbarity of the white American. And, as if he anticipated an argument from me, he launched into a full account of the indignities suffered by the African at the hands of the barbarian, chief among which was having to take on the imperialists' god. The other staff members nodded their approval, but, concerned that I might take offense, hastened to assure me of their good will toward *this* "barbarian." Especially since they had expected a white volunteer. After which, shaking hands all around, we relaxed.

One other noteworthy event for me at this party: whenever a woman guest arrived, everybody, as if by automatic control, stood up and remained standing until she was seated. All talk stopped, regardless of the intensity of the conversation. I was terribly impressed by the dignity of it all. Never saw anything quite like it in Half Assini (or in America, for that matter).

OCTOBER 6

Every time I go to town I notice something new. Today it's a library, a community center, and the largest apartment dwelling I've ever seen anywhere in Ghana—a five-story building occupying one whole block.

The place is buzzing with religious goings-on: the Apostolic Church, the Christ Apostolic Church, and a couple of other smaller splinter groups in full swing. Drums and tambourines, filling the air with small thunder,

143

sounding exactly like those "sanctified" revival church meetings my mother used to drag me to in big-foot country. Only these people were in mourning.

Apparently Half Assini isn't the only place where cat is considered not only edible but a delicacy—a fact that continues to send shivers down the American's very proper back. *The Voice of Ethiopia* is up in arms because a PC volunteer, in an article for his hometown paper, claimed that "fat pussy cats" are a *standard* part of Ethiopian diet. (The old "ghosts and animals" crap again!)

Funny, this time I felt just a little bit ahead. A few years ago, when I traveled the route—Japan, Guam, Canada, England—courtesy of the Air Force, I too had blinders on to everything but that which had more than a little "shock value." Today, all I can remember about Japan is the gonorrhea I picked up there ("you ain't a man till you've had a dose"); England—the fog, and a remark dropped by a bus-ticket seller, who "don't like monarchy." But Ghana had me with my eyes wide open, and I wouldn't forget anything about her for a long, long time . . .

OCTOBER 7

Found a pile of journals on my desk this morning, including the *British Weekly News* and the *Ghana Teachers Journal* (wihch is distributed to the kids as well). I guess the *American Outlook* is next . . . The English teacher I met at the party the other night tells me proudly that all kinds of sophisticated material can be found in the library—*Ebony, Readers' Digest, Time,* and several romance-type sheets from the USSR. I had gone to his place to borrow some beer and incidentally was attacked by a virtual blanket of insects. Couldn't escape the damn

things, even when he let me in: all the windows were wide open, and hordes of them clung to every piece of furniture in the room. I watched his kids, busily engrossed in a game on the floor, and his wife, sitting calmly with her youngest on her lap, and couldn't believe my eyes: none of them seemed the slightest bit aware of the myriad wings beating the air around them.

OCTOBER 8

In a tour of the school's poultry farm today, I counted twenty chickens, thirteen ducks, four goats, and several rabbits. From what I hear, local snakes are responsible for keeping the number of animals relatively constant. Part of the farm has been reserved for agricultural products, but here several mistakes have been made. The orange trees, for example, yield a fruit about the size of a stunted grapefruit, with a cauliflower-like covering, and it tastes like a lemon.

OCTOBER 10

The Peace Corps field officer dropped off a footlocker of books from Washington—a *permanent* gift to the school. No wonder—each one is a greater repository of propaganda than the next. I lugged the damn things over to school just as communal service was letting out (wonder how my colleagues feel about my absence: they all attend), and was stopped by the education instructor. He teaches English at the missionary hospital and wanted to know if I would be willing to teach their nurses-in-training biology one hour a week. Sure—it's no sweat off my ass . . .

So, the school keeps a record of the students' religious and tribal affiliations. While in the lounge, I overheard the teacher in charge of registration ask a student his religion, and the student replied that he had just switched from Anglican to Moslem. The teacher, putting a few more questions to the kid and apparently being satisfied with his sincerity, noted the information in a record book and also on a large bulletin board. Interesting: I had always thought the "conversion" of the non-Christian to the Christian was much more the order of the day, but I learned otherwise in the course of this afternoon.

"How I Spent My Summer" can't hold a candle to "One Day in the Seminar for Teachers, Students, and Voluntary Leaders of the Ghana Young Pioneers, Berekum: Theme—*Education and Citizenship.*"

First to arrive, with an entourage of eight in a chauffeured Chevrolet station wagon, was the Berekumhene, the town chief—a big, broad, bald-headed fellow wearing gold-trimmed sandals and sporting a huge gold ring. As chairman of the affair, he introduced the first speaker—the Berekum D.C., a youngish man, plainly dressed, with a great flourish of a moustache and a speech that was equally to the "point": those who fail to see education as a means of furthering the best interests of the state are no better than enemies of the state, and should be dealt with in like manner.

Our principal followed him with a rather elaborate discourse on "citizenship" and what he called "psychological imperialism" (in preference to "colonial mentality"). The African has rid himself of colonial rule, he said, but not of certain attitudes instilled in him by that administration. Those currently at work putting roofs on the school bungalows, for example, are "lazy, totally non-competitive," still nursing a hangover from the days

146

when they had a set income that made it impossible for them to rise above a certain status. They hadn't worked to optimum capacity then, and they weren't doing so *now*. "Today the government is ourselves. There is no white man on top. Lazy people are enemies of Ghana." He wasn't talking about those "too old to be reformed" but about those young enough to know better. Teachers had their task cut out for them in helping to define those talents useful in the service of the "community" (and not "state," because, as he confided to me later, he thought politics and education should be separate). "When we serve Ghana," he said in conclusion, "we serve ourselves. When we serve the world, we serve humanity."

The next fellow spoke on "The Role of Teachers in the Ghana Young Pioneer Movement," giving a brief history of the organization and some of its early difficulties, notably the naming of a staff. At that time, leaders had to virtually beg teachers to volunteer their services: today it is the teacher's recognized duty to play his part in the movement. And just as he is trained to teach academic subjects, so must he be trained in the proper ideological idiom if he is to be an effective dispenser of Nkrumahism. Subjects at these training centers cover "fear of God" (loud laughter, because the YP was once accused of being atheistic, like their Russian counterparts), "love of country, and foot drill," as well as the learning of "patriotic songs," and "crafts and games." The teacher is reminded that, since no special classroom period is set aside for YP activities, he must "intertwine" them into his regular lessons.

There are several means at the teacher's disposal for adjusting the school program: during English period, for example, he can make "additions" of certain pertinent literature to the syllabus, and ask the children to compose simple poems wherein Nkrumahism may be the

theme. In arts and crafts he can direct the children toward an appreciation of African culture per se and the "struggles of the dynamic CPP" in particular. They might do a series of paintings depicting Osagyefo as prisoner, Leader of Government Business, Prime Minister, and President. Ghana's history and geography can be emphasized—though not at the expense of other countries' history.

Last but certainly not least, every morning the teacher should take two or three minutes for a lesson in ideology, perhaps starting with one of the tenets of the YP Code, such as "Love of Country." This so that a child, the next time he goes to town, will buy Ghana matches instead of foreign ones. But one must be careful lest he unknowingly "defeat the ideology." If a child in music class stops singing to admire a photo of Osagyefo on the wall, don't rebuke him. "Tell him that you are aware of his love and that you too love Osagyefo. But Osagyefo likes children who sing, who do their work."

The next two speakers, the Regional Party Education Secretary and the Deputy Minister of Communications and Works, Mr. Bennah (also Member of Parliament for the area), were dry as dust by contrast—textbook type lectures. Only the difference between their reasons for supporting socialism was of interest. The Secretary quoted from *Socialist Morality,* in which Osagyefo defines as a society that in which each is his brother's keeper, while the Minister stated that, unlike Britain, France, and the U.S.A., Africa has no private capital for development. Both equally questionable foundations on which to build socialism, it seems to me.

(Incidentally, the Minister is currently under heavy attack in the party press for his "anti-socialist" tendencies!)

The last speaker was to address us on "African Unity,"

but he dwelled at length on Ghana's independence in·
stead. A true independence, but not ever to be taken foi
granted, because "the imperialists are always on the
alert for an opening in the United Front of the people."

The chief finally stood up and urged those in attendance
to join him in bringing the seminar to an end: "Long live
Osagyefo, long live the CPP, long live the Ghana Young
Pioneer Movement."

OCTOBER 13

Went to "Cherry" party last night in honor of departing
Regional Commissioner. No cherry served. Beer and
Pepsi. The Russians were there in force—a haggard-
looking group, with two or three women among them.

The English teacher made some nasty comments about
the guest of honor—par for the course. Said he's extrava-
gant, buys a new car every month. Waited for the big
boys to arrive, though I don't know why. The bigger they
are, the duller the party—guess no one was in a festive
mood after sitting through the seminar. Only the Russians drank and were merry. We just drank.

OCTOBER 17

The principal tried to impress me with the benefits
Ghana stands to derive from her policy of non-alignment.
I wasn't impressed because, as far as I'm concerned,
any non-alignment other than of a political nature is
merely a figment of the Ghanaian's imagination. He has
no idea how *much* he is aligned with the "Western way."
His commitment can be seen everywhere: in the design of
his modern buildings, the books he reads, the religious
attitudes he expresses, the clothes and cars he wants to
buy. And it is the *source* of the influence here that is sig-

nificant, not simply the objects themselves. The Ghanaian wants particularly those things the people in the United States are believed to enjoy, and even goes about getting them in much the same way. Even African socialists are not unaware of a certain "Westernism" in their thinking—a statement that made the principal blanch. What the hell, I shouldn't tease the guy: he takes himself so seriously.

OCTOBER 18

Made the rounds with the vice-principal last night, finally winding up in a nifty little bar where my friend translated some Ghanaian high-life songs for me. One dealt with the evils of rumor-mongering: "Tell others only what you see with your own eyes, not what you hear with your ears" (da-de-da-da), "Don't talk against the party unless you've experienced injustice from it yourself" (doo-ah). Jesus, I never realized before how far the government's gone to spread its message! And with the installation of television they'll have covered all fronts. As Nkrumah said the other day in Parliament: Ghana TV will not cater to cheap entertainment but will "reflect completely our culture, philosophy of life, and national objectives."

At about 11:30 P.M., just as the bar was closing up, we witnessed a curious scene: a gang of what appeared to be young toughs dressed in straw skirts and strange masks parading down the street. The bartender said they were vigilantes: seems that quite a bit of rape, robbery, and destruction of property had been going on the past few weeks, and since the police couldn't or wouldn't curb the crime wave, the townspeople had taken matters into their own hands. I later learned that not one rape or rob-

bery occurred after these guys put the heat on (for a long while, anyway).

Went to a lecture co-chaired by the principal and an American who makes his home in Britain—"that Anglicized American," the principal calls him. The guest speaker, a white Englishwoman on the President's staff, spoke on nationalism in Africa, beginning with an incredibly long and boring account of Livingstone's "discovery of Lake Tanganyika and Victoria Falls" (which brought understandable groans from the students).

When she finally got around to the subject of discrimination, citing Ghana as an excellent example of a country that enjoys "racial harmony," the principal sprang from his seat and shouted, "There is no racial harmony, we simply tolerate white people here" (which brought the house down). "Only when the black man everywhere rediscovers himself, his identity, will there be racial harmony." Afterward a few of us went to his house and over a few beers he recalled with a stinging cynicism how, while he was studying in England, British university students would pelt him and other African students with snowballs, calling them *all* Mau Maus. His earlier comment during the lecture no doubt stemmed from the wound left by this incident. We talked a little about the lecture, but inevitably the subject of domestic politics reared its ugly head, and we were off on meatier matters soon enough. Everybody but me blasted away at the Nkrumah regime. The English teacher said he should have stepped down a few months after his first term as President and ruled from behind the scenes, like Mao. He would have been a hero. Now his cult has its hold on him and will eventually destroy him. Someone else said

he has a friend who's close to Nkrumah, who smiles and fawns on him but denounces him in the company of trusted friends. And then, for some strange reason, the English teacher jumped in with a remark that was way out in left field, about PC girls "doing anything an African asks them to." The others just stared at him with blank expressions, but he jabbered away, taking them apart piece by piece—and directing his anger toward *me* all the time! When he finally landed on a volunteer I knew—a white girl—and accused her of being a "Goddamned bitch spy," I nearly squared off, but instead slammed out of the place.

It took me a long time to calm down, but when I did, I saw two possible reasons for the poor slob's outburst. One, he had been loose-tongued when he showed his contempt for the administration in front of *me*—a member of the Peace Corps and, as such, supposedly working hand in hand with that administration. Two, he was obviously preoccupied with the white girl he slandered. Maybe he had made a pass and been rebuffed. Or just maybe he hates himself for *wanting* a white girl. Well, whatever it was or is, I'm not having any—even if it means an isolation booth for the rest of my stay.

OCTOBER 20

I guess when Ghana said she would have nothing to do with South Africa, she meant it; over lunch today, the agriculture teacher told me he had been taking a correspondence course in watch repairing from a school there, and when the boom fell, not even that was allowed. Boycotting her all the way. I wouldn't put any money on her if other countries follow suit . . .

I don't know what it is, but every guy and his brother seems to be desperately interested in whether or not I

believe in God and what denomination I am. I was sorely tempted to tell my friend I'm "a twenty-dollar bill," but I'm glad I kept my mouth shut: he obviously takes his gods with a little more than a pinch of salt. After lunch, as we were strolling back to school, he pointed out a large, beautiful shade tree near the campus entrance, remarking that before the school was built, the tree had been a center of traditional worship—a shrine where people would bring sacrificial offerings to appease the gods. Many believe that ghosts are still lingering about—one reason why, when the contractors wanted to cut it down, they vehemently objected. I was amused to see several students sitting cross-legged under the giant, leafy branches, rapt in their texts, some of which no doubt queried the validity of sacrificial practices!

OCTOBER 21

After browsing through the library all afternoon, I'm happy to report that, contrary to what certain skeptics believe, Ghanaian schools are *not* "inundated" with communist literature. In fact, I found only *six* Eastern periodicals, compared with about 150 publications from Western or pro-Western countries—Japan, England, America, West Germany, India, and, of course, the majority from Ghana. When I opened the folder containing *Russian News,* the first headline I saw was: "Russia—the Last Imperialist Power." Ha! What a joke: one of the student librarians had evidently mistaken the American propaganda sheet for a Russian newsletter.

On my way back from town, I stopped in at the Methodist Book Store to compare, and noticed several copies of *Animal Farm* displayed prominently on the shelves. Obviously the government hasn't curtailed commercial sales of the book. The clerk says it's selling like hotcakes.

I didn't stay as long as I meant to, because a commotion was going on outside, and even the clerks ran out to see what it was all about. A big crowd, mostly kids, was gathered around a fellow demonstrating and selling teddy bears that rocked up and down and blew up balloons. One was black and had representations of charms around its neck, wrists, knees, and stomach. I had never seen teddy bears in Ghana before, and, from the thrilled expressions on the faces around me, they hadn't either.

Incidentally, talking about "mistaken impressions," I thought I'd mention that I dispelled a few the phys. ed. teacher had about us volunteers—in particular, the "sacrifices" we had to make, all in the name of Ghanaian progress. No washing machines, dishwashers, a murderously inefficient public-transportation system, lousy pay, etc. Well, I soon had him feeling sorry for himself! Compared with many a Ghanaian, the volunteer lives like a king. At least 90 per cent have cook stewards to wash their clothes, clean their houses, and prepare their food. As for transportation, those who have to travel long distances to stores or hospitals are given a vehicle and an adequate petrol allowance, and any repairs are paid for by the Corps. Medical care is free. And while our salary may be less than what we might get back in the States, living expenses are much lower here. In fact, some volunteers save as much as 40 pounds a month out of an allowance of 58. Sure, we don't like ants, mosquitoes, and other lousy insects, but then we're not crazy about them at home, either.

Last but certainly not least, how many of us would have saved 1,500 clean C notes over the same period of time at home, especially those of us who recently graduated from college? No, the volunteer's lot was a relatively happy one, unless, like me, he was particular about the company he kept!

Reading old issues of *Drum*. I didn't know that Negro American dentist Robert Lee was the first to naturalize, or that he was one of only three or four such cases. I remember hearing something about how, after being in Ghana for some time, he went home to visit his southern relatives, had enough of a look around to see that things hadn't changed for Negroes, and rushed back to Ghana to become a citizen.

I wonder what the Afro-American head of the Ghana State Insurance Corporation thinks about naturalizing, now that an assemblyman in Parliament got all hot and bothered yesterday about his having the post instead of a Ghanaian. No, I shouldn't think the Afro-American has much call to feel secure here: I'll bet when the ax of Africanization falls, white *and* black outsiders will find their wings clipped.

I read further that Lee went to school with Nkrumah. Well, I'm sure damn few Negro Americans would be out here if it weren't for their personal associations with the Osagyefo . . .

Now, remembering last night's talk with some of my colleagues, particularly their reaction when I asked how they thought a biology instructor should approach the subject of sex. Was really thrown when most of them said, Tell them anything but the truth, even if they happen to see two dogs mating and ask what they're doing. I must have looked horrified, because they stumbled all over themselves trying to explain that when they were kids the subject was taboo, and anyone foolish enough to even mention the reproductive organs brought on himself the wrath of the gods. So much for the Western view that African kids, being allowed to watch everything their parents do, are sexually liberated. True, up to a certain age they walk around naked, but not because of any lack of

sexual restraint: in fact, quite the contrary—there's a strong streak of Puritanism in the Ghanaian, quite apart from that which comes as a result of learning the "Christian ethic."

The vice-principal said that when his two-year-old asked her mother, during the last pregnancy, why she was so fat, the mother said that she was eating too much. After the baby arrived, the loss of weight was attributed to eating less; and the baby came from the hospital. Now what's so strange about that? he asked me. Didn't we tell our kids that babies come from the stork or God?

Having got over this hurdle (though with some sweat), we took up that second great equalizer: money. Not only how to get it but where to *keep* it. A clerk at the Bank of West Africa had told me he thought the Ghana Commercial Bank was riddled with corruption, the result of a fluctuating currency, and I'd be better off doing business with a British-owned firm (his, of course). The vice-principal was in full agreement with the clerk and excused his savings account with the Ghana bank as a gesture of loyalty, nothing more. I remarked glumly that if it came down to losing money, I'd rather an African and not a European outfit bear the blame. His attitude irritated me—the Ghanaian wanting nothing more than a national identity, yet, when things got tough, withdrawing his "confidence" from his home bank and investing it with the foreigner. And it bothered me just as much when, as the party was breaking up, he told me to drink up, since the one who provides the booze (and I had) should always take the first and last shots. Americans, I recalled, also had a saying like this: the one who takes the first swig from a bottle takes the "poison off." What was our No. 1 loyalist thinking of, then? African poison—or American?

Back to today: on a plant-classification expedition around the compound with my first-year biology students,

156

I was viciously attacked by an army of giant red driver ants. I don't know why, because they were being bitten, too, but for some reason the kids found it hilarious, especially whenever I cried out in pain. Even though I had on long pants, the fugging things somehow withheld their bites until they had gone up my legs and massed on my ass and other sensitive parts. Dropping everything and shouting with agony, I rushed to the john and stripped to the bone . . . They'd have to forget about field trips for a while—a *long* while!

Meanwhile, back at the school everybody was all shook up, but not by ants. The new yearly budget had been announced over the radio, and there was a substantial tax increase. As a colleague explained it, Ghanaians, unlike Americans, are just not accustomed to paying taxes, and even a slight increase makes them feel as if they're being robbed blind. (Sounded pretty much like home . . .)

The teachers were particularly incensed at the jump in automobile tax, particularly on those assembled in Ghana. It just didn't make sense: the Ghanaian in general had little enough to live on before, but now that he'd be levied for the car that might make all the difference between a poor job and a good one, he might as well throw in the towel altogether. There were the big guys, sitting on their tax-free asses, driving tax-free cars, while *they*— teachers, clerks, day laborers—sweated it out to cough up "just a little more" each year.

When I told them they don't know how lucky they are, that in the States one has to pay many more kinds of taxes, they looked at me as if I was a cancer victim talking to a pneumonia victim, sure that my affliction would get me before his got him.

They had another beef, too, I discovered, not about the "government" but about the "people." It seems that in some areas of the country, children still think it's a bless-

ing to have yaws, and parents actually force them to associate with whomever has the contagious disease. And the kids cling to another superstition, equally hard to dispel—that thieves and ghosts will come in if they leave their windows open at night.

OCTOBER 23

According to *Spark*, Nkrumah has turned down a multi-million-dollar offer from a foreign businessman. While he liked the idea of a metallurgy firm in Ghana, he *didn't* like the condition that all the shares would be in foreign hands. Seems like a precipitous move to me: why should a foreign power consider pouring capital into this country in the future, when other African countries are just as needy but less particular? Surely Ghana could use the increased employment such a project would mean, also. Oh well, I'm just one of the "people." What do I know? . . .

Later, when I happened to ask the principal what he thought about it, he condemned the action outright. (As I suspected, the guy's definitely anti-party.) But I found out something else about him, too: just as strong as his contempt for the new administration is his denial of an "African personality" as conceived of by the party. It's no more than a political gimmick employed by those who have recently thrown off the colonial yoke and are looking for a hook to hang their nationalism on. Surely *fu fu* pounding and drumming are peculiar to the African culture, I suggested; but he replied hotly that some people in Pakistan pound food in the same way, and as for drumming, only the talking drums are uniquely African, but then not all groups use even these. Even the kente cloth is Ashanti-derived. "Well, then," I said slyly, "if Africa, traditional Africa, has nothing peculiar to herself, then Africa has nothing unique to offer the world, right?" I

had him there: he was about to admit no such thing. Of course there are "cultural patterns" in Africa; all he meant was that no line can be drawn between what is *only* African and what is not. Besides, he added, what made me think that in order to be valued, a culture must necessarily be unique?

I didn't dig him. Here he was making a case for the "mythology" of the African personality, yet, when I suggested that many foreigners shared this view—that Africa has made no original contribution to world civilization—he jumped down my throat.

Well, obviously he doesn't like being compared with his oppressors, but what he doesn't realize is that, to gain the respect of the world, Africa has to respect herself—and this means all the way.

OCTOBER 24

So, there are a few points at which the principal's views coincide with the official party line, whether he likes it or not. In a speech to the students today—UN Day—he mentioned that, while visiting a school on a routine inspection tour, he heard a teacher asking the children to recite "Pussy cat, pussy cat, where have you been? I've been to London to see the Queen." Whereupon, there and then, he told the teacher to go to England, for he wasn't a citizen of Ghana. The point being that, though the words mean little in themselves, "this is cultural imperialism at its worst." (The Minister of Defense had once made the very same argument, claiming that the rhyme was "very loaded" and should be changed to read, "Pussy cat, pussy cat, where have you been? I've been to Accra to see Osagyefo at the Flagstaff House.")

Also, like many a party stalwart, he was highly critical of the role played by the United States in the UN.

159

Like Russia, she was in it only for what she could get. Britain and France, too, deviating only on small procedural matters from their once benefactor (the Marshall Plan). How could the UN claim to represent all nations when, just because the United States said so, China was excluded and Formosa seated? Apparently the Declaration of Human Rights applied only to white men when it was written. Or else "some were more equal than others."

As to how effective the UN actually is, those agencies concerned with maintaining peace can do little when they mainly serve the interests of the United States, and they do, "because the U.S. controls a disproportionate number of votes." Countries like those in Latin America have no choice but to go along with her: the hand that feeds the mouth will withdraw the food if the mouth doesn't open properly. Africans are welcomed and allowed to say their piece, but they don't really have a deciding voice, especially if it is in conflict with the "Voice of America." Thus Africa must rid herself of all special-interest blocs other than her own, and exert herself not through eloquence but through action.

He concluded by saying that the UN can best serve the interests not of power but of peace by acting to free people from all special interests and pressures of oppression —all people, not just those prescribed by U.S. foreign policy. But he wanted the students to understand: he was simply giving them historical facts, not preaching hatred of the white. "Africans would probably pursue the same policy if the positions were reversed. It is human nature for the strong to dominate the weak," he said.

OCTOBER 27

Tired of sitting around. Nothing to do. Town is dead. Sad but true—where there are people, there isn't always life.

Bird calls and mongoose wails are swell, but they're not car horns. No, I need some good old city-type noise, and though Kumasi's not Accra, it will have to do—even if only on weekends.

Catnapped. Dreamed of hamburgers. So real that I almost beat it over to the mission nuns to see if they might have any good chow. Incidentally, they've decided that a nun should teach biology to the student nurses after all. I wonder why they changed their minds.

OCTOBER 28

Now the ed. teacher tells me the nuns *want* me to teach. What the hell! First they say yes, then no, then yes again.

Bill of lading for the shipment of some books I ordered from Alpha Phi Omega arrived—158 boxes with twenty-five books each. Quite a haul. The Brothers are all right. Too bad I can't do Northern Illinois a good turn. If only I knew how to preserve specimens, I could send them a "rare" collection of insects and flowers . . .

OCTOBER 29

A big roar of approval in the staff room over speeches in Parliament critical of the new budget. No one can tell me that Ghana doesn't have a vigorous assembly, or that the party doesn't allow differences of opinion within the organization to be aired: many of those with the most cutting remarks are CPP. And although it has nothing to do with me, I'm happy too: one of my students penned a few lines on the blackboard—and they're *good*:

> O Solitude, where are the charms
> that sages have seen in thy face?
> Better dwell in the midst of alarm
> than reign in this horrible place.

Passed a couple of hours thumbing through old copies

of *Drum*. Get a real kick out of a 1953 issue, in which the editor asks: "Should there be intermarriage between Africans, coloreds, and Indians?" Must have been a safe question, because South Africa took up its publication that year.

Up to 1953, little of a political nature appears: mostly articles on gangsters, foreign travel, model citizens, boxers who made millions (and lost them, like Joe Louis), "unknown" Indian South African millionaires, comic strips that try the imagination, and of course a sizable ad section—cure-all medicines, bleaching creams, hair straighteners, etc. But, by 1954, *Drum* is carrying "all the news that's fit to print": articles galore on the South African nationalist movement (interesting to see how active the clergy is in politics) ; columns crammed with new phrases—"Christian love," "white and black brother," etc. (the Christian missionary did a bang-up job!) . And two years later the September issue has a lead article on Nkrumah, including this comment on his eating habits: "He probably doesn't eat meat because of his upper artificial teeth." Hell, I have an upper and I eat meat. And at this moment I'd give all my lowers for a good pork chop!

OCTOBER 30

Big ruckus in staff room over letter from the party's local steering committee demanding 5 per cent of the salaries of all party members. (Some staff members were quick to claim no association with the party.) Also up on the bulletin board was a list showing the breakdown of the students' religious affiliation:

Roman Catholics	38
Anglican	10
Presbyterian	36
Methodist	54

Seventh-Day Adventists	3
A.M.E. Zion	2
Jehovah Witness	1
Bethany	1
Salvation Army	2
Mozoma Disco Christo Church	1
Cherubim and Seraphim	1
Moslem	10
Total	159

No professed pagans in the school!

Once back in my room again, I pulled out some more issues of *Drum*—this time to brush up on the now defunct opposition party. A high-ranking member makes this statement in 1958: "The United party thinks the State exists for the individual. The CPP, on the other hand, thinks individuals exist for the state." Appiah, another big mouthpiece (now on ice in detention), says: "The United party when in power will tend to orientate to the West while having diplomatic relations with all other countries." The United States must have really dug the UP.

Also found a speech made by Nkrumah to the African Women's Conference in 1960—perhaps the most poetic words he ever uttered:

> Women of Africa, yours is the duty and privilege of hoisting high the nationalist banner of redemption; yours is the glory of answering the call of our beloved Africa; yours is the enviable opportunity to call a decisive halt to the ruinous penetration of colonialism and imperialism in Africa; yours is the honor to fight relentlessly for the total emancipation of this great continent; yours is the task of projecting the African Personality to the world of today . . .
>
> It [1960] is the year of the climax of the revolution in which Africa has rebelled against the shame and injustice which for so long has been meted out to her. The clarion

163

command echoes across the mountains and the valleys, across the rivers and the lakes, across the oceans and the deserts: Hands off Africa!

The Negro American and West Indian delegates must have been as touched as their African friends and hosts.

OCTOBER 31

I can't explain it, but I have the queer feeling that things are going to explode in this country. Disquietude rampant. The place is overloaded with complaining Ghanaians, and it makes me very uneasy. As I said to the phys. ed. teacher earlier in the day, Ghana is one big experiment, and many of Africa's little people are watching to see whether she succeeds. I don't know how she can when even her own people don't trust the government they chose, and judging from the leadership, I'm not so sure I don't sympathize with them sometimes. The budding Navy, for example, like the Air Force, is dominated by British officers who have proved untrustworthy in times of crisis. Why the government keeps them on I don't know: just as I don't know why it continues to have confidence in the masses (who are, to anyone not blind, obviously discontent).

NOVEMBER 2

Have been sitting in the library rummaging through some copies of Ghana's parliamentary debates. Interesting how consistent the opposition is in their criticism of every bill CPP members bring to the floor. They're at each other's throats even over basic issues of foreign policy, social justice, and African unity. One can understand why the ruling party felt that the UP was too much of a

thorn to tolerate. But I wonder if they know how much the opposition speaks for the middle-class Ghanaian.

I might add that the debates are not without a certain amount of humor—to *this* observer, anyway. All's fair in love and war, and apparently in "socialism," judging by certain remarks made by the Minister of Justice at one session. He was well into an analysis of the benefits to be derived from a socialist state, commending Ghana's efforts in that direction, when suddenly a member interrupted him to shout "One man, one car!" The Minister paused, looked a trifle disconcerted, regained his composure, said, "Yes, one can't ride in two cars at the same time," and took up where he left off. Well, I've personally seen five cars parked under his raised house, at least three of which (I'm told) are his. Later, he amended his earlier statement by saying, "If a man has two cars, there must be a need for them."

NOVEMBER 3

One of my students just brought me some tiger nuts from town. Sweet—like English walnuts. He says they arouse sexual desire. Well, about the only thing I feel any passion for today is getting back to the debates! . . . I pick at random, and find a nice, juicy row over whether Nkrumah's birthplace should be made a national monument now or later. Only one CPP man raises an objection to the "now" motion, saying that the birthplace should be "preserved after the man is no more." An opposition fellow agrees, pointing out that the statues of great men in Europe were pulled down immediately after their deaths or ouster. "Nkrumah must surely recognize the folly of allowing himself to be so commemorated while he is living." The Leader of the House reminds them of one rather signifi-

cant fact: "Nkrumah *has* objected, but was overruled by us."

By the way, I'm amazed at the number of titles used to refer to Nkrumah in these sessions:

> Osagyefo
> The Right Honorable
> Founder of the Nation
> Fount of Honor
> Our Messiah
> President of the Republic
> Commander-in-Chief of the Armed Forces
> *Font et origo* of the State of Ghana
> Head of the Order of the Star of Ghana
> Head of the Order of the Volta
> The Leader
> Doctor (several honorary degrees)
> General Secretary of the Party
> Life Chairman of the Central Committee
> Chancellor (of the three universities)
> Kantamanto (also the name of a gin)
> Moses of Africa
> Head of the Black Star
> Initiator of the African Personality
> Veranda Boy

Jesus! I don't believe one member of parliament's argument for supporting a January 1962 bill (States' Secret): "If one listens closely enough, a new note may be heard in the *Nation's* song. [my italics]. This new note runs:

> 'Oh my country, 'tis of thee
> Sweet land of freedom and justice
> of thee I sing
> Land where our fathers toiled . . . ' "

She even ends the thing with "Let Freedom Ring"!

166

Still on debates. September 11, 1962—motion to make Ghana a one-party state introduced for the first time. It's mystifying to me that it comes from a former opposition fellow. . . . Ha! I didn't know that the United States once loaned Ghana four technical advisers to help set up the Workers' Brigade. At that very time our papers were denouncing it as "communist inspired and infiltrated."

Taking a break, I had a great workout on the tennis courts and a swell dinner afterward at the geography teacher's house—fried plantain, cassava, and cocoyam leaves cooked with beef. The mosquitoes were out in full force, but even they couldn't ruin it for me. Which reminds me—in a recent speech, Nkrumah said that 80 per cent of all disease in this country is malaria. Another statistic comes to mind, this offered by an M.P. in the House in May 1962: ten thousand deaths caused by malaria alone in one year, a figure that prompted this response from another member: "Some time ago there was a motion before the House urging the eradication of mosquitoes. At that time I opposed the motion because the mosquitoes were not attacking me, but now the mosquitoes have turned against me. . . . First, we have to congratulate the mosquitoes on their gallant stand against the white man in this country. . . . It is unfortunate, therefore, that we now have to destroy the mosquito. But we must destroy the mosquito because its enemy the white man is gone and it has become a nuisance to us." Probably brought the "House" down . . .)

Ah, if only my little friends in the bathroom—the lizards—would eat mosquitoes instead of the meaty beetles they squash all over my wall . . .

167

Big hullabaloo in staff room again: today's the day the House approves or rejects the Preventive Detention Extension Bill. The teachers are unanimously con, and apparently so are most of the M.P.'s, though one never knows *what* they really think. I'm reminded of an incident recorded in the debates some time ago, when an M.P. moved that the House express its appreciation of the work done by the Workers' Brigade. Only the Minister of Defense and the Leader of the House said aye; the nays won hands down. Yet, strangely, when the Minister called for a head count, only one—repeat, only *one*—member voted against the motion; and, even stranger, this one turned round the very next day and said he had in fact voted *for* it! There was much checking and cross-checking, and it was finally determined that the man had voted *against*. Why deny his vote?

Had two good letters today, one from Ocran, saying he's applied and been admitted to the Ideological Institute. (He's already complaining about the work load; I can see why—political science, political economy, Nkrumahism, government, statistics, French, English, African studies, constitution, and philosophy.) The other from a volunteer stationed in Togo. God, a letter from there takes as long—five days—to reach Ghana as one from the States!

Klu, the music teacher, was just telling me the most incredible story about spirits and ghosts on the campus. It seems that the first principal of the school drowned in one of the school wells, and his "spirit" has been haunting the compound until quite recently, if one is to believe his successors, each of whom has "seen" the spirit in the

bungalow reserved for the principal's use. Klu says that when they literally began to run away from the school with their families, the Ministry brought in certain fetish priests to drive the spirits away. Interestingly enough, there was one principal in this long parade who had so much "strength" that the spirit stayed away from him. Klu says *he's* too strong for them, too—but he looks as if he's not so sure about me!

NOVEMBER 8

It seems that someone else fears the core of Nkrumah's government is full of pits. The November 1 *Spark* says of Parliament: "In the first place, nobody questions the right of the opposition members to challenge both the provisions of and the political philosophy behind the budget." But, "While opposition members can criticize details to the extent of rejecting the principles of the budget, the government members can criticize the details only in order to strengthen the socialist principles behind the budget." In other words, CPP members must, like some of my Christian friends in Half Assini, refrain from questioning the foundation on which their ideology rests.

Yep—I'm now convinced that it's all got to crumble one of these days. I can just see it: Kwame Nkrumah Market in Kumasi changed to Asantehene Market, Nkrumah Circle in Accra changed to Ga Manche Circle . . . Too many forces arrayed against you, Kwame: the missionaries whom you should know care nothing for socialism of *any* variety; your own vanguard party men; those coming from your universities and secondary schools; Indian, Lebanese, Syrian, and even Ghanaian merchants. The battle is uphill all the way, and not even a *mild* socialism is to be won at the top. You'd rather die than give in to capitalism, but surely you can't hide long

169

from the fact that the private sector of your economy is the most virile and productive . . .

Nor will you be able to assure your country of an increase in American capital invested solely on your terms. The United States might just be biding its time until you're forced to seek investments from inadequate sources—Russia, for example—so that they can rush in with a huge infusion of marshaled capital, thus demonstrating the superiority of "free enterprise" over "isms" other than their own. I'll just bet they wouldn't be so noncommittal on the idea of a political union of African states if all African governments were sympathetic to, say, the ICFTU (International Confederation of Free Trade Unions)! Beware—"We want for the Africans what they want for themselves" may not include the Nassers, Ben Bellas, and the Nkrumahs who also have mandates to rule from their own people.

NOVEMBER 9

Cannons were going off all night long, booming today's funeral for the chief's wife. All staff members are obliged to attend. At a meeting this morning it was decided that the school's contribution to the funeral would be 5 pounds. Only the phys. ed. teacher objected, on the grounds that "such excessive expenditure on funerals should be discouraged"; but this was "one aspect of African culture" the principal wanted preserved.

And preserved it was—in booze.

What a gala affair. The chief must have cramps from shaking the several thousand hands of all his well-wishers. The Queen Mother, too, who must be approaching one hundred. Together they sat on the concrete, he with a bundle of grass clenched in his teeth as a sign of mourning, and watched the mourners pass by in their

funeral attire—brilliant orange, blue, red kentes—to the strains of two high-life bands (probably there especially for the youngsters, who were dancing gaily all over the place). A traditional drumming crew placed in a prominent spot drew the elders and culturally inclined.

Truly a day of celebration. Both men and women dipped freely and uninhibitedly into the gin pond to toast the admirable number of donations received by the chief. Unfortunately, I thought of a few other things to toast as well, and had a walloping headache when I got home!

Later, the principal came by to tell me that a girl he was supposed to see tonight had died right after the funeral of an internal hemorrhage. A recent operation had left her in no state for the festivities, and she had overexerted herself.

NOVEMBER 11

Klu showed me a list on which his music students had written their favorite performers—Pat Boone, Fats Domino, Little Richard, Elvis, Cliff Richards, Chubby Checker, Joe Turner, Brook Benton, the Everly Brothers, and Nat King Cole! I don't know why he's so depressed. I mean what kid *anywhere* digs Maggie Tate? . . .

NOVEMBER 12

Picked up a pamphlet on the Young Pioneers today—for those back home who might be leery of any communist ideology lurking between the lines. As one can see (unless he's determined to see otherwise), the spacing's pretty tight:

INSTITUTIONALIZATION SLOGAN
Leader: Nkrumah does no wrong.
Response: Nkrumah is our Leader.

Leader: Nkrumah does no wrong.
Response: Nkrumah is our Messiah.
Leader: Nkrumah does no wrong.
Response: Nkrumah never dies.

PLEDGE OF THE GHANA YOUNG PIONEERS

1. I sincerely promise to live by the ideals of Osagyefo Kwame Nkrumah, Founder of the State of Ghana, Initiator of the African Personality.
2. To safeguard by all means possible the independence, sovereignty, and territorial integrity of the State of Ghana from internal and external aggression.
3. To be always in the vanguard for the social and economic reconstruction of Ghana and Africa.
4. To be in the first rank of men fighting for the total liberation and unity of Africa, for these are the noble aims guiding the Ghana Young Pioneers.
5. As a Young Pioneer, I will be a guard of workers, farmers, cooperators, and all the other sections of our community.
6. I believe that the dynamic Convention People's Party is always Supreme, and I promise to be worthy of its ideals.

AIMS

1. To train the mind, the body, and the soul of the Youth of Ghana, to be up to their civic responsibilities so as to fulfill their patriotic duties.
2. To train their technical skills according to their talents.
3. To foster the spirit of voluntarism, love, and devotion to the Welfare of the Ghana Nation.
4. To inculcate into the Youth "Nkrumahism": ideals of African Personality, African Unity, World Peace, Social and Economic reconstruction of Ghana and Africa in particular, and the World in General.

CODE

1. Love of Country.
2. Discipline and Obedience.
3. Honesty and Morality.
4. Punctuality.
5. Protection of State Property.

6. Reliability and Secrecy.
7. Comradeship and Forebearance.
8. Love of Work.
9. Field Craft.
10. Unaffectedness.
11. Self-Control.
12. Striving to Faultlessness.

INSPIRATION OF THE GHANA YOUNG PIONEERS:

"Place the young at the head of the awakened masses. You do not know what strength, what magic influence the voice of the young have on the crowd. You will find in them apostles of the new social order. But the youth lives on movement, grows great by example and emulation. Speak to them of country, of glory, of great Memories."

Dr. Kwame Nkrumah, 1948

NOVEMBER 13

Had a date with a chick last night who told me more about the girl who died at the funeral. It seems that she had a premonition of her impending death, because she told friends that she had been visited by a spirit—her deceased mother—who asked that she "come home to heaven," but, in answer to the girl's pleas, granted her one more day to enjoy herself. The day of the funeral was thus to be her last. My little chick must have believed the story, for she wore a string of charms around her waist under her dress and wouldn't take it off even in the bedroom.

NOVEMBER 14

Small get-together at the principal's house—the vice-principal, ed. teacher, geography teacher, and I hashing out Nkrumah's now famous slogan: "We prefer self-government with danger to servitude with tranquility"

over a bottle of Ghana gin. My colleagues were of the opinion that Ghana wasn't "ready" when granted independence, and therefore Nkrumah had no business pushing it. As far as they were concerned, they couldn't see that it had changed things much, anyway. When the geography teacher asked me what Ghana produces now that she didn't in 1957, my first response was "cigarettes," but he pointed out that the company is foreign owned and managed. I then mentioned tennis shoes, which he accepted but grudgingly: they were so poorly made that only a week's wear and the soles were hole-ridden. So I switched to the new schools going up everywhere, but he came back with, "They're half empty." At this moment the ed. teacher interrupted with an old standing joke about Nsawam being for "people who talk like" the geography teacher. Not being in on it, I treated the comment seriously. But how the hell was I supposed to know he meant Nsawam *prison,* not *cannery!*

In retrospect, I have to admit that they're right: very few Ghanaian-produced goods and services have been added since independence, but then Ghana won't be built in a day, either . . . no matter how impatient her people.

NOVEMBER 17

Just thinking how great the general atmosphere around here is. I have my own bungalow, comfortable furniture, and privacy—which means when it gets too damned stuffy, I can walk around naked without "alarming the neighbors."

Spoke too soon. Almost broke my wrist smashing a mosquito against the sturdy, guaranteed-privacy concrete wall. He's engraved there: killed in the line of duty, approximately 10:00 P.M., 1963. Crushed by overwhelming odds. May its soul rest in peace. And be a warning to all others!

174

Broke a tooth this morning while washing my denture. Brought it to school to show the kids why they should take good care of their teeth. "You don't want *false* ones, do you?" I said, pushing it partly out of my mouth. They jumped back in horror.

On to the staff room and another battle of wits (but I probably flatter myself). This time "they" were on the side of "free enterprise," and I was plugging for "collectivization" (or at least a clear understanding of what is meant by both, without preconceptions and bias). I'm sure they never know what to make of my "anti-Western" attitudes, but at least they stop and pause and take stock of their own positions.

Off the battleground and home, where I picked up a note left in my door by one of my students:

THE BANK OF TRUE HAPPINESS
Pay   mr. eddie c. smith   or Bearer
the sum of Three Hundred and Sixty-Five Happy Days, Health and Prosperity in the New Year.

It's a bit early but appreciated.

In one of my fourth-year classes I was saved from a possible dose of sleeping sickness by a student who saw a tsetse fly about to bite my leg. He lunged from his seat and gave it the old death stroke. The fly's appearance always causes a big commotion in class. When we had all calmed down and got back to the lesson, one of the kids asked why it is that when a pregnant woman is hit or slapped, her baby will oftentimes have fingermarks on its face in exactly the same place. Or if she is cut on the arm during pregnancy, the baby will have a scar at birth

on the same arm and in the same location. I was really stumped, because he said this was no superstition, he actually *knew* of such cases, and judging from the class's response, so did they. I don't know why I'm still so dubious. Hasn't the Mayo Clinic got stranger things on the books? . . .

NOVEMBER 21

I read in *Life in Modern Britain* that English ministers have an income of about 5,000 pounds a year. I wonder if Ghana's counterparts realize that their salary is 100 pounds more per annum than their former masters.

NOVEMBER 22

It's got to be some kind of horrible joke! Kennedy dead? But I know it's not a joke, and so does everyone else—his murderer best of all. Why won't the tears come? Am I afraid they wouldn't stop? . . .

> Farewell beloved one
> Farewell O mighty warrior
> Farewell, rest in Peace.

> South, North, a hundred years ago
> Lovers quarrel: never
> Shall thou end?

> O captain, my captain
> Protector of right.

> O constitution?
> O Christianity?
> Oh . . . America.

> O mighty fallen Western Star!

Forgive me, Whitman, for the crude imitation . . .

176

Had a lousy night's sleep, jolted out of bed by night-mares—or was I awake and only wished they were night-mares? Couldn't seem to pull myself together: it was as if part of me was back there, in that hell called home. God, how terrible to be there now . . . but terrible here, too.

I walked around in a daze, looking for someone, any-one, to talk to. Would these people I had come to know just a little understand why I grieved? Would any of them feel the loss themselves, for their own reasons? Two Canadian teachers at school—just as chipper as if nothing had happened. The principal—asked only what I thought of the assassination. The phys. ed. teacher—what would have happened if the murderer had been a Negro? Kunii, the geography teacher—eating when he heard the news, couldn't finish, "loved Kennedy like a father" . . .

NOVEMBER 24

Klu and a few others here, including an African priest, are convinced that a conspiracy is responsible for Ken-nedy's death. They seem almost as grief-stricken as I, and somehow I don't feel so horribly alone any more.

Even the poet McNeill Stewart, whose verses usually resound with anti-American sentiment, is in mourning today: the government paper carries his tribute:

ON THE DEATH OF PRESIDENT KENNEDY
He rode in pomp, pride, circumstance and state
Into the cruel jaws of cruel fate;
Into the cold, remorseless arms of death,
While millions stunned with horror held their breath!
A hush fell on the world, deep as a prayer;
And with each sigh there came with grief—a tear!

177

O, what a price to pay for liberty!
O, what a sad and bitter destiny!
The end was sudden! O, but what an end!
This Kennedy was freedom's greatest friend.
He loved, no matter of what race or creed;
His was the noblest love of all indeed—
A love no man could ever sell or buy;
A love intense—a love that cannot die!
When shall we ever see such love again!
Now he lies there, numbered among the slain!

As we look back on all the grand array,
When he was made the first man of his day,
And all America, with one acclaim,
Paid him a tribute that adorned his name.
We see that nation, born in liberty,
Honor her son with pride and dignity.
With pride we watched him start his great career;
Resolute, hopeful, honest, without fear,
A dedicated man to freedom—peace,
Resolved that racial hate and wars shall cease:
Eager, within life's little measured span,
To vindicate the brotherhood of man!

World tension, with master-hand, he helped ease;
Where there was discontent he soothed and pleased;
Firm in his task, but mild, he played his part,
And won a place in every human heart.
He was a man of courage, strength and worth,
Whose presence gave a new hope to the earth.

His journey o'er: the laborer's task is done:
A nation lays to rest a noble son.
Among his great forefathers let him lay;
Hallowed shall be the spot that holds his clay—
A spot where youth, through each succeeding age,
Shall ever make a solemn pilgrimage.
And, there, beside his silent, solemn shrine;
Seek inspiration in a faith divine:
Not only youth, but men of every clime,

Shall find new solace in this spot sublime—
This consecrated spot where liberty
Is one in faith and God with Kennedy!

NOVEMBER 28

I was walking home from the office this afternoon when
I heard loud popping noises coming from a nearby tree.
I thought at first it might be a bird of some sort, but then
saw that it was seed pods spontaneously cracking open.
An amazing sight. I also noticed that the vulture tree is
shedding leaves and beginning to bud flowers. Most of
the vultures have abandoned it for a nearby alternate.
I shivered. The season must be changing, for the air is
much cooler—temperature must have gone down to 50
degrees last night—and the window screen was clear of
insects for the first time.

DECEMBER 2

USIS traveling salesman Twitty—an Afro-American who's
on a tour of English-speaking African countries demonstrating a NASA space wagon—gave me several copies of
President Johnson's message to Congress and photos of him
and Kennedy. My Ghanaian friends somehow got wind of
the gift, and all, including teachers, laborers, clerks, and
bartenders, rushed in pleading for copies. Principal later
put some up on the bulletin board, and I noticed students
standing three or four feet deep to take a peek. Good.

Also good that a young man had an ideal, and I and
millions of others are a living testament to that ideal.

DECEMBER 4

Just had a good talk with Klu, during the course of which
I asked him about the "character" of his people (think-

ing that he'd give me some insight into the practice of human sacrifices). Either he didn't understand my question or was purposely evading the issue. He talked instead about his deep admiration for the Germans (who had once controlled that part of Togo that is now eastern Ghana), particularly because they had instilled "discipline and love of excellence" in his people. And of course because they (like him) were music lovers. I tried to pull his attention back to my original question, this time asking him outright if he knew of any tribes that still made human sacrifices. Again he skirted the issue, flying off on a tangent about how his people (Ewes) have always been looked down upon by other tribes, particularly the proud Ashantis, and cited as an example a story told him by the principal, an Akwapim. The principal had once brought a Ewe classmate home with him for the holidays, to his parents' great indignation. Was this the best companion their son could find? But their guest bowled them over with his dignity and charm, and they begged him to accept their hospitality next vacation. (I'm surprised they didn't expect him to "detribalize" himself!)

The third time I put the question to Klu, he gave me a direct answer, but not without some discomfort: "It's less true in Eweland than in Ashantiland. Of course, human sacrifice was once widely practiced. The Ashantis still do it when a chief or other big man dies: he needs a servant in ancestor-land." I was about to push it further, but one look at his sullen face and I asked him how he was doing in economics: he was taking a home-study course, and sometimes came to me when he couldn't solve a problem. He looked relieved, and eagerly recounted the problem that was currently plaguing him: "If the price of cheese goes up, what happens to that of butter?" What a foolish question to ask a Ghanaian: a

foreigner would immediately go to the source of both—the cow—but there are few cows in southern Ghana, so how can a man like Klu be expected to figure out the answer to a problem so remote from his experience? But then these courses, devised by foreign institutions, are naturally foreign oriented.

We later stopped by my place and listened to the Negro spirituals playing on the squawk box. For a few moments we stood and hummed together on the porch, and then Klu bounded down the steps and into the insect hums of night, shouting back over his shoulder, "America is too free. That's why things are not quite right. There should be more of the traditional German self-discipline —not to the extent of militarism, however." (I'm glad he added *that* . . .)

DECEMBER 7

Here's an eye-opener: *Spark* calling *Ebony* an "instrument of imperialism." When I showed the headline to the principal, he shook his head emphatically. "They're right," he said, "blacks trying to imitate whites, that's all." Is that what the Negro volunteer was doing in Ghana? Trying to make like a white? And how about the AMSAC (American Society of African Culture, a largely Negro American group of scholars interested in Africa)? Is that merely an "instrument of imperialism," too? *Spark* seems to think so, although they're not blaming the Negro per se. Rather, the Negro is all too often blind to the fact that he is being used: it is assumed that because he is black, the "African will readily accept him." And here we've been thinking all the time that America's finally opening up and beginning to hire us because we're *qualified*. Now we're told that it's simply *expedient* for the U.S. government to have black faces in

conspicuous places to do the white man's dirty work . . . Interesting that the editor makes it clear that his paper does not represent or speak for the government!

Some white American diplomat must be having a big fat laugh over it all. So many birds killed with one stone. Negroes given more jobs, easing racial tension at home, not because the most articulate segment of the Negro community is finally being recognized, but because by removing them from the plight of the masses, the white man is also straitjacketing effective leadership. The Negro needs spokesmen for his cause, and if they're all busy pursuing new-found careers, the movement is slowed down, and it's that much harder to gain the ground they need to win. No doubt about it: the Negro's always caught in the middle. If he's a valuable pawn in diplomatic maneuvers, he's a suspicious commodity to the African, because "one bad apple spoils the barrel." (Like Fred, who, you will remember, beat up his wife, bringing disgrace to his company in the Brigade.)

What a world. Perhaps it's best after all to see things either black or white, with no shades of gray . . .

DECEMBER 9

Great to be in Accra again. The minute I arrived, I beat it over to my Ga friend's house to find out how the treason trial was going, and whether a verdict for the three former ministers had been handed down yet. Right while I was there it was announced over the radio: all three had been acquitted and were to be released. Ha! What a joke on Ghana's enemies! Here was "freedom and justice" handed to them on a platter . . . the government prosecution, led by the Attorney General himself, worked hard to convict these men, and now it seemed there was an independent judiciary after all!

The trial has everybody jittery, glued to the radio waiting to hear what the government plans to do about the verdict. The PC field officer says things "are pretty tight. Internal revolution could come from the right as well as the left."

I got my third tetanus shot today. Thank God! The doc also tells me I've got what looks like an *amoeba* in my blood. Two other volunteers have, too. Jesus, maybe we'll go down in medical history—but I'm not ready to go just yet!

DECEMBER 11

Went out to the university bookshop today, and who do you think I met? None other than Half Assini's sometime-principal-in-residence—Ackah! He bent my ear for an hour, moaning over the fact that only six Ghanaians out of a student body of twenty-one are in the master's program in African Studies; overseas students from Europe are in the large majority. Afro-Americans must be better than nothing, I guess, because Ackah's still trying to convince me to apply.

Other stops I made today included a "ruffian" tavern with my Ga friend, where I kept expecting a "rumble" to break out at any moment, and a quick search at Flip and Flop's (two Afro-American chicks) for some "illegal" Johnnie Walker to take back to Berekum for Christmas . . . God, Accra's about to burst at the seams; the trial's on almost everybody's mind, and the tide seems to be running against the government, especially after today's dismissal of the Chief Justice, who was presiding judge. I'd hate to be in Nkrumah's shoes now: it wouldn't make much difference which shoe you put on which foot—left or right, neither would fit!

Good lecture tonight—"Chieftancy in Modern Ghana"—
by the Dormanhene, chief of the nearby border village in
which I teach an extension biology course, and a research
officer in Nkrumah's office. Talked more about the party,
though, advising the attentive audience to think of Ghana
and other African single-party states not as "one-party"
governments but as "nationalist movements," consisting,
as they do, of diverse tribes and peoples under one roof.
Thus there is no reason for anybody "to be outside the
party." As for where the chief's loyalty should lie, during colonial times he was no more than a caretaker in
charge of "native authorities." He had to serve the interests of his overlords, not those of his own people—a
fact that, during the struggle for independence, found
him, albeit involuntarily, aligned with the colonialists.
But times had changed, and so too must the chief—or be
left behind. "The most important thing for him now is to
jump in and help his people with self-help projects."

I thought the questions that followed were most pro-
vocative. C.K. wondered whether there was in fact a *need*
for chiefs within the socialist framework. The chief replied that "many people, especially those in rural areas,
still look to the chief as their father, the embodiment
of their culture, their very life, their link not only with
their ancestors but also with modern administrators."
Hopefully, people will take their problems to, say, district commissioners in the future, but until that time the
chief must continue to serve as their focusing point.
"Without this symbol of stability and continuity to guide
them, their lives would be meaningless." (He completely surprised me: I was sure he was going to hold
up the chief as one example of traditional culture to be
preserved.)

The Berekum D.C. asked if he thought the govern-

ment should continue paying the chiefs "retainer fees": surely the money would be better spent on local councilors, since they receive no pay and do more than their share of the work. The chief agreed that the councilors should be recompensed; but to cut off the chief's allowance would be disastrous, since they have little other means of subsistence.

One student asked why, when a new chief is being installed, he runs into the bush, and is beaten by his people if they catch him, and got this reply: "He wants to know whether the people really want him." If he is chased, he is presumably wanted. Another student raised the question I had asked Klu earlier: Is a human sacrifice made when a chief dies? He was told that, in Ghana at any rate, the practice is no longer followed, contrary to what certain misinformed people believe. Only animals are sacrificed now, and maybe that too will soon disappear.

The one question in all our minds, and the last of the evening—how was it possible for the trial to go the way it did?—also puzzled the chief. Traditionally, the executive, judiciary, and legislative branches of government, like everything else, were in one man's hands—the chief's—and it was hard to believe that a case backed by the Chief of State through his "elders" and advisers could be thrown out by the judges. If the Court had at least informed the President of their decision before making it known to the public, "he would have had time to prepare the people" (or reverse the verdict?).

DECEMBER 24

Ah . . . the day before Christmas, and all through the House—bedlam! Nkrumah's Christmas message to the

185

nation: all the proceedings and judgments of the treason trial are "null and void."

Returned to Berekum last night. The tension in the air was electrifying. Everybody grumbling about the trials. C.K. ranting against Nkrumah, claiming that, because of him, Ghana's lost her leadership in Africa to Ethiopia. Jesus, doesn't he know the *Economist* (where he picked up this info) represents the West and would be the first to welcome the ascendancy of the "moderate" Emperor as the leader of Africa?

DECEMBER 2 7

Christmas Day was a dreary affair—everyone too down in the mouth to celebrate—and unless something extraordinary happened (a complete change of heart, for example), New Year's wasn't going to be any different. So, the morning after, not nearly as hung over as I had hoped to be, I took off for Accra. If I was going to mope my mid-semester vacation away, I wanted to do it with a bang, not a whimper!

Had dinner with Flip when I arrived, and heard all about her sad love life. Seems that her Ghanaian dates are only interested in getting her to bed. "Just like home," she said: they didn't want to marry her, either. Flop, her girl friend, didn't have these problems: she wasn't "ready" to get married just yet.

Quiet holiday. Decided to stay in Accra till school reopened.

JANUARY 2

So far, an uneventful holiday—that is, up to today. I was sitting in the bar across the street from the hostel this afternoon when a guy rushed in and announced that

Nkrumah's aide-de-camp had been shot. A few minutes later, another guy ran in and said it was Nkrumah's *driver* who was shot. The 6:00 P.M. news announced that an "unsuccessful attempt" was made on the President's life as he walked to his car: one security guard was killed. I left my stool, where I had been glued for several hours, and walked a couple of blocks, hoping to hear something I might have missed on the radio, but nobody was talking—to me, anyway. Groups of people were clustered in front of doorways, whispering, but when I approached them, they suddenly stopped. You couldn't be too careful these days—especially when it came to "foreigners." And all I could get out of Boss Carter was that he could no longer sympathize with the present administration. What *was* clear to me, and what nobody needed anybody to tell him, was that at least *one* person had decided to stop grumbling and *do* something. How long before others followed his example?

JANUARY 6

School reopened today, and all the kids wanted to talk about was the attempt on Nkrumah's life. It seems as if this one incident had to occur before people would vent their anger openly. The principal, for instance, was all for using violence to overthrow the government, whereas before he had merely whined like everyone else. The dismissal of the Chief Justice was the last straw, he said. Up to that point Nkrumah had all the cards, but he had tipped his hand and the people weren't going to be bluffed any more. The ballot box was a farce; "civil liberties" a pacifier; "justice" a catchword. The man had to go, and his advisers as well—even those who secretly disagreed with him—right down to the D.C. and anybody else connected with the party. (I silently wondered if

both the principal and C.K., who had gone to college on government, therefore party, scholarships, considered *themselves* eligible for the hangman's noose!) He even gave a blast at black people from the the Americas: "They come out here with their slang and stand solidly behind the regime." But, angry as I was, I forgave him his outburst: he was at least 50 per cent right.

JANUARY 8

The Regional Health Officer stopped by the school today to say that the Regional Steering Committee has changed its original demand of 5 per cent of staff salaries for the party building in favor of a flat 40 pounds. The principal replied hotly that all contributions would be voluntary, not mandatory; but later he urged everyone—laborers, kitchen help, clerks, etc.—to give something "so we can keep our daily bread." (Incidentally, the R.O. seems to share the principal's view that the time has come for "violent action." "Nkrumah doesn't know Ghanaians. He's not a Ghanaian. He was away from Ghana too long.")

JANUARY 9

Today's papers carry news of more dismissals of civil employees. (The teachers are rejoicing and saying the "last coffin has been nailed." . . . That's one cliché they got ass-backwards.) Also a run-down on those who sent "congratulatory messages" to Nkrumah on his escape from near-death. None from Western leaders . . .

During a bull session in the staff room, the principal said there was a Positive Action rally yesterday at which the man sitting next to him—an agricultural officer—confided that if Nkrumah were to be killed, he for one

wouldn't ever want to see a President with so much power again. He no doubt was thinking of 1959, when Nkrumah could walk the streets protected only by masses of market women.

JANUARY 11

The First Secretary to the Russian ambassador is due here for a speech tomorrow, as the ambassador is unfortunately too busy with pressing matters to come. (Probably keeping tabs on Chou En-lai, who's here in Ghana.) The Secretary will be staying at my place. Jesus, wait till he sees all those pictures of JFK and LBJ over his bed . . .

JANUARY 12

Well, the First Secretary made it, vodka and all. Gave a pretty articulate speech, considering his poor command of English. But maybe I should say he got his point across despite this major difficulty. Talked almost exclusively about economics: what production was like before the Revolution and how changed after; who owned land then, how many more owned it now, etc. (information that can be got from any history text) . And obviously he hadn't anticipated any hissing—which was the response when he said that there is no unemployment in the USSR—for he ended his talk abruptly and left the room. The staff persuaded him to return, and there followed a rather lengthy question and answer period. The Secretary obviously *had* anticipated what questions would be asked, however (they were always the same) . As to whether a bloody revolution is the only means of achieving a socialist society, he said the conditions in each country and the will of the people determine what

form the struggle takes. On the precepts of Christianity as practiced in the USSR: "As for me, I'm an atheist." What he considered the relationship between socialism, communism, and Nkrumahism to be: he could speak only on *his* kind of socialism: "Other peoples and countries will have to decide their systems and directions," a reply that brought audible murmurs of approval. But the consensus of opinion among the staff seemed to be that the lecture was "worthless" because it "excluded the human factor." I personally wish someone had asked the fellow about Hungary, since he had pointed to Czechoslovakia, Bulgaria, and Poland as countries that had known a "bloodless revolution," but I dared not ask myself: I'd be on the next plane out if the PC thought I was "involved" again.

A little later I checked the library to see what the Secretary had left: several books—Lenin, Marx, and Engels, Khrushchev—many more pamphlets, mostly of a technical nature, and a few short-story collections. Too bad most of them will sit and collect dust on the shelves

JANUARY 14

One thought and one only prompts this entry, as I put the wraps on my third notebook. Whatever else the "essential Ghanaian" is, he is a Western man—a fact often underemphasized by anthropologists and other experts on African culture and politics. As with any people who have been long subjected to another people's rule—be it imperialist, colonialist, communist, socialist, or what have you—it is nearly impossible to tell where one complex leaves off and the other begins. I, for one, see a configuration as clear as any in the sky: tribal-American-Ghanaian-English.

JANUARY 15

This semester's going more smoothly, though I'm not sure why. The Ministry of Education prohibits volunteers from teaching educational psychology, but, God, I'd have practically nothing to do if *no* compromises were made.

Bananas from the school farm were on sale today, but all were gone before I got there. It does the old ticker good to see the kids being rewarded for their back-breaking work. Yams, cassava, oranges, etc., have been harvested and sold since I've been here. It's always a thrill to see the boys rushing past my house about 5:30 A.M. on their way to their small individual plots.

JANUARY 29

I notice that the *Graphic* has announced its new board of directors—appointed by Nkrumah! That about completes the takeover of the mass media. I guess the party **is** supreme!

JANUARY 31

Like the man says, trouble's a-brewin'. The U.S. embassy has been accused of spreading rumors against the government. Picketers out in front of the place all day. The joint is really jumping. Clipped this piece from the *Ghanaian Times*—for future reference (and it looked like my "future" was just about here).

> MRS. RABBIT ADANKOWAA
> *Sweeps to Reveal*
> Whether the time is
> not overdue for the
> crime and vice squads of
> the police to swing into
> action and save young

Ghanaian women who are
at the mercy of loiterers,
Western spies, parasites,
C.I.A. agents, Peace Corps
scoundrels and women
hunters who have polluted
the atmosphere of relaxa-
tion and jollity at the Lido,
Metropole, Ringway and other
night spots, and
whether it will not save
the nation's honor and
reputation if an all-out
assault on crime and im-
morality should spread
into the night clubs parading European decadence
and corruption in the
name of entertainment at
the Cassanova and other
shady night clubs.

FEBRUARY 4

Much has happened in the past few days. The principal
was furious when he found out I was writing a diary, and
demanded to see it (I'm still stalling). My colleagues and
I had a bitter falling out, and my senior biology class refused to take one of my exams. Where can I possibly go
from here but up? Or are there layers of hell that, when
peeled off, reveal still another, like an onion?

FEBRUARY 6

The demonstrations at the embassy are still going on.
Probably why classes were canceled today. The staff is
definitely fraying at the edges.

I hear that my favorite bar, the De Africana, is closing shop. The locals suddenly decided that the bartender was a "suspicious character" (he's not a native of Berekum) and stopped patronizing the place. Mrs. Rabbit's bites? . . .

FEBRUARY 10

Better stick close to my own little anthill. Papers have it that six university lecturers have been dismissed and deported—a West Indian, a black Frenchman, and four Americans (all white). Accra getting hotter by the minute. One embassy officer, an Afro-American, "heroically" raised the American flag after it had been lowered by the demonstrators, thereby eliciting the censure of the *Times* for his "foolishness": such an act could only arouse the crowd to greater violence and further alienate the African and the Afro-American (probably the idea!).

A number of Russian engineers from regional headquarters stopped by the school this afternoon. Loaded with cameras. Funny how they seek out only Ghanaian members of staff on these now-frequent visits . . .

Can't tell what my students really think about what's happening. They're still talking about the "big cars and plenty money" in the States, but somehow I feel a challenge in their eyes now. Or is it that they see one in mine? . . .

FEBRUARY 12

It seems that prices are skyrocketing. Students are complaining about the increase in their boarding fees. But the school is being charged more for food: flour up from 1/18 to 2/14 a bag, sugar up to 7/12 from 2/0! Most surprising of all, cooking oil is up from 32 to 40 pounds per drum: isn't the new Nzima Oil Mill producing enough to stabilize prices?

193

The papers report that after this contract expires, Ghana will not ask for another Peace Corps contingent . . .

I'm still not on speaking terms with my colleagues. More on it later when it's safer. To hell with them, anyway. All I want to do now is split this scene.

Today's *Times* carries a reprint of a letter it purportedly received from a group of Afro-American sympathizers in Berkeley, California, and above it the editor's comment:

WE SUPPORT GHANA

Twenty-eight Afro-Americans in Berkeley, California, have expressed their unqualified support for the actions Ghana took in dealing with subversive elements in Ghana. In a letter to the editor of the Ghanaian Times the Afro-Americans condemned, vehemently, the disgraceful behavior of Emerson Player, an Afro-American "diplomat" at the U.S. embassy in Ghana during the recent demonstration at the embassy.

Dear Brother-Editor—
We, as Afro-Americans, deeply regret the traitorous actions of Emerson Player and the other "Uncle Toms" from the U.S. whom the Ghanaian government has intelligently expelled from Ghana.
Let us assure you, brother, that there are innumerable Afro-Americans—and we who are writing this letter are among the most militant of them—who not only despise these traitors, but unqualifiedly support the actions and attitudes of the Ghanaian government *vis à vis* the imperialistic, anti-black U.S. government.

Yours for the Liberation and Unity of all Africans.

194

Hard to believe that the paper would cook up such a story. Probably true, if interesting . . .

FEBRUARY 19

Radio Ghana reports that more heads have rolled. A minister and two deputies got the ax.

I closed my savings account today.

FEBRUARY 20

Seems like the papers are really doing a job on us. The story of an American ten-year-old who gave birth to a child really splashed across front page: "Only in U.S." Reporter carried away: "Immorality, burglary, racial discrimination and murder cases are some of the social vices rampant in the United States." Well, my friends, twelve-year-old Ghanaian girls give birth as a matter of course. Does two years *really* make that much difference? Besides—an unimportant little fact, I know—such cases have occurred in many other countries, as long as you're interested . . .

FEBRUARY 22

Out of hell for a day, five hundred miles away from Berekum. Was given permission to travel with the school hockey team to Pusiga, which is quite near Kulungugu, site of the attempted assassination. People are still talking about it.

My first visit to the north. Low, round mud huts in scattered compounds, wide rolling plains with few trees, and endless stretches of land barren from want of use. The

195

wind blowing in over the grasslands makes me think of Montana.

Walked into town with some of the students. Hot, dry, and dusty. Couldn't even get a beer. Moslem influence? No stores as such, just a market that opens every three days. Everything dusty; sores on children. But ah! Those endless stretches of landscape; and the wind howling across the tops of the long grass, the herders with their hump-headed cattle spotted here and there . . . Only half a mile from the Upper Volta–Ghana border.

But it *is* pretty desolate. I wonder who ever dreamed of putting a secondary school here. Must be new, because it's constructed of concrete block, whereas the training college where we're staying has dorms patterned after the traditional mud huts. No, a Ghanaian didn't suggest the design, the school was built in pre-Independence days. The principal is a European, and though I haven't met him, he must be an unusual character to relish spending so many years in the company of nothing but miles of endless nothingness.

And here it was, in remote northern Ghana, that I saw an almost naked woman for the first time. She wore only a G-string, and, to my amazement, the students laughed as loudly as any "civilized" bigot from the "south."

FEBRUARY 24

When I got out of bed yesterday morning in Pusiga, my leather shoes wouldn't go on my feet. The dry climate had shrunk them—sucked the moisture right out. Guess the people who live there (and can afford leather shoes) buy them several sizes too large. But what do they do when the rainy season comes along, and the things expand?

On the return trip, the students were so thirsty that they

drank out of the Volta River when we reached the ferry. Not this kid—no river blindness for me!

FEBRUARY 29

I'm going to Accra tomorrow to ask for another transfer. Six forty-five-minute teaching periods a week is ridiculous, especially with only ants, cockroaches, and mosquitoes to keep me company in all that leisure time. Besides, the water situation's as bad as it was in Half Assini, and these pit latrines stink something awful.

MARCH 9

Have been in Accra several days, sharing the apartment of a young English pharmacist I met through some volunteers a while ago. Nice guy but lousy friends: all Corps. More conservative in *every* way than when they left Berkeley.

While in the PC office trying to secure a transfer, I overheard a phone conversation between the Ministry and the boss: the principal had reported me to the police as "missing in action." The s.o.b. is just trying to be silly: to hell with him!

MARCH 16

The one thing I continue to care about in Berekum is the school farm. Now that I've been appointed rural science advisor, I get down there at least once a day.

Today I concentrated on a half-inch-wide column of red ants moving swiftly through the forest. The kids showed me how they build their homes in trees, like birds. One would never notice the nest unless he had a keen eye and knew what to look for. At first look, it appears to be

197

a spider hideaway—several leaves shaped in the form of a ball with webs holding it intact, usually in orange trees. The students handled the little beasts like trained biologists, even allowing themselves to be bitten to show me how the stinging apparatus works.

They also pointed out some of the signs a farmer looks for to determine the approach of the rainy season. When he hears the popping of certain seed pods, for example, he knows for sure the rains are not far off, and immediately begins to plant his crop. Like true Eagle Scouts, the boys pulled the leaves from certain trees and bushes and explained how these, unlike others they mentioned, could be boiled and eaten. I was even shown how to extract starch from the cassava plant (the same used in starching clothes).

MARCH 17

The PC Field Officer dropped by today to see if he could smooth things out between me and my colleagues: we'd been on the outs too long, and the principal had now added *his* voice to those against me. The bastard had led the officer to believe that the "clash of personalities" was simply too great for the situation ever to be any better. When "goody two shoes" put it to me, I confirmed the majority vote, adding "Fuck 'em!" (I don't think he was pleased.)

MARCH 18

The ed. teacher slipped me a copy of *How to Win Friends and Influence People.* The fink.

Did a cop-out and visited the mission hospital for a change of pace. Boy, those nuns can certainly talk up a storm. One thrust some propaganda pamphlets into my

hand, claiming that the Church was the only way to salvation for these "children." Why, only yesterday two chaps had been brought in from the bush after each had nearly butchered the other with cutlasses. One will die; his hands were completely severed, and a shoulder was left dangling from its socket. (They didn't have to be so goddamned explicit!)

MARCH 19

Letter in the *Evening News*:

AFRO-AMERICANS WANT TO RETURN HOME

Dear Editor,

We are the same group of relatives who wrote you in the fall of 1962. We, as of this date, have not succeeded in our efforts to return to our motherland, Africa, but we have made some preparations we believe will make us more useful when we get there.

Six young men in our group have completed nine months of technical-electronics course. Plus two of the young ladies will have completed a course in typing and shorthand. As of now we have an experienced machinist with twenty-five years of experience in this field.

We are determined to find a way back to our motherland. We realize that there are many of our people in America that don't realize that in going against Africa, they are in fact going against themselves.

We feel that we are blessed to recognize our true heritage and culture in this land of turmoil and confusion. You must realize that 90% of the black people in America have been brainwashed against Africa. There are a few groups in this country who connect themselves to Africa by "lip service" only, because these same people would not be willing to go to Africa today, but if the opportunity presents itself, we would be ready to leave today.

There are fourteen adults and eleven children in our group. We are a very close family and we all would like to

stay together. Although we are all hard-working people and have worked all our lives, we have never been able to save any money. We would like to come over on contract or some sort of work program. We plan to stay once we make it there. Our only difficulty is in getting transportation.

We are writing this letter exploring every avenue in order to know by the completion of our courses just how and when we will reach Africa. Any information you can give us will be greatly appreciated.

Sincerely,

God, if they only knew what the African's true feelings were toward the Afro right now, they'd sooner write to their *own* government!

MARCH 22

Time running out for me, only two weeks to go.

MARCH 26

A Seventh-Day Adventist stopped by today and asked me to exchange for Ghana currency a $5 bill somebody in America had sent him. I whipped it out, no questions asked. Never knew the old bill could feel so good in these fingers.

MARCH 29

Went to a dance last night in Sunyani with the ed. teacher; I sat in a corner and smoked four packs of Tusker cigarettes, but even minding my own business I managed to annoy someone! When the Regional Party Secretary happened to pop in, everybody rose but me. He gave me one of the dirtiest looks I've ever seen—actually glowed with silent rage. Jesus, I didn't think he'd take it so hard. But I've been mistaken about a lot of things lately.

In the library today I came across an old issue of the *Marxist Review* and nearly flipped over two items played up in bold type:

> The U.S. rulers are pinning hopes on the activities in Indonesia of the Peace Corps, which as everyone knows, is a widely branched-out organization for ideological subversion and espionage.

> When this issue [Dec. '63] had already gone to press, the whole world was shocked by the news of the tragic death of John Fitzgerald Kennedy, President of the United States. Communists, being utterly opposed to terror as a method of political struggle, are outraged by this foul murder, and extend their profound symapthy to the people of the United States. The assassination of this outstanding statesman is a political act which benefits only those ultra-reactionary elements who are opposed to peaceful coexistence of states with differing social systems. Together with all sincere people everywhere, the Communists condemn the violence let loose by the reactionaries in the U.S.A.

Hmmmmm! "Opposed to terror," eh? . . .

In Accra again. Keep coming back like a song . . . Had a pretty good time with a West Indian and his Swedish wife, and a South African nationalist married to an American white girl. All Marxians and sympathetic to Mao. The South African quite bitter about what he calls "the treatment African refugees get at the hands of the Bureau of African Affairs." Says "Sure, they'll give our top exiles big cars, a hotel room, and spending money, but few get to see Nkrumah." Even the top man in Swaziland's nationalist party, recently arrived from talks in London,

couldn't get in to see the Leader, and left in a pretty big huff.

This particular exile hasn't been able to find a job since arriving in Ghana, and lives off his wife's teaching salary. She's quite a girl in her own right: born in Angola of American missionary parents, has a degree from an Ivy League college, widely traveled, taught in many African capitals, and knows personally quite a few top African Marxists in Conakry, Dakar, Accra, etc.

We all made it over to the Caprice for a couple of drinks and were busily chewing the fat with a few other exiles when the manager suddenly removed the band to another floor just below us. Nobody in our group thought anything about it, but a guy sitting near us—a young Ghanaian broadcaster of South African music for Radio Ghana— took the act as a personal insult and showed his anger by drumming loudly on the table with two forks. All hell broke loose: some mountainous dame, probably the manager's wife, rushed the kid and told him to get the hell out. He laughed in her face, and she responded with short rights and lefts to the head. He hit her back, which brought all the waiters and the manager to her defense. Chairs were turned over, bottles broken, glasses smashed. He was lucky they didn't throw him off the roof!

We kept cool: none of us could afford to get involved.

APRIL 12

Had a talk with the new PC director before leaving Accra (Boss Carter's done flew the coop). He said I could leave immediately after our termination conferences in May or any time after the first of June without suffering any repercussions. I've decided to try to stick it out through June.

APRIL 13

Radio Ghana reports that Malcolm X is arriving tomorrow for a tour of the country. If the *Times* is any indica-
tion of the reception he'll receive—three or four lines
tucked in an obscure corner on the back page—I don't
think he'll stay long. (The *Evening News* didn't even mention his visit.)

APRIL 17

Somehow picked up the dysentery bug while sleeping on
the South African's living-room floor. Poor guy—he got
a really bad dose. Says the U.S. embassy must be keeping
the arrival of Malcom X a big secret, if he came at all!
He and several Afro-Americans went to the airport to
meet him, but he wasn't on the plane.

My school had given me its blessing to pick up a shipment of books the PC had sent from Washington, and I
was amused to discover that the Ministry of Foreign Affairs had censored such titles as *Making Modern America, From Immigrant to Inventor, Babe Ruth, Exploring
Literary Trails,* and *English and Continental Literature*
and substituted instead *Alice in Wonderland, Treasure
Island, Call of the Wild, Little Women, Tom Sawyer,
Black Beauty, Heidi,* and *The Prince and the Pauper.* Of
course, there were the usual number of science and math
texts as well.

Several of my colleagues and their wives came by to
say thanks for the books, and C.K.'s wife even invited me
to lunch tomorrow. Guess they've changed their minds
about me, but I won't count on it. Once burned . . .

APRIL 20

Hopped a lorry for Sunyani just to break the monotony,

and ended up giving a couple of speeches at the primary schools there. Several teachers, when they learned of my arrival, approached me and asked if I would tell their kids about life in America. I did, and this time my heart was a little more in it: I had definitely decided to leave Ghana in early June.

APRIL 24

Just as I was leaving the staff room today I nearly stepped on the head of a monster snake lounging just outside the door. Well, this was one ugly thing I wasn't about to preserve for my biology class, so I smashed his head in with a heavy wooden ruler. Later I learned that this was one of the most poisonous types in the country, and the mortality rate from their bites is extremely high. Found another one just twenty yards from my house. Cripes, the damn things are certainly showing a lot of guts these days. Have to keep the doors closed from now on: wouldn't want to make it home on a crutch. Come to think of it, wouldn't want to *not* make it at all!

APRIL 25

I've always wondered about Hanna Reitsch, head of Ghana's gliding school. She's said to be a close friend of the President's; now I read in *The Last Days of Hitler* that she was an intimate associate and follower of Hitler's and was with him in the bunker right to the end. It's a big, wide, wonderful world . . .

APRIL 27

At a small get-together at Kunii's house tonight, his wife gave two demonstrations, one of her culinary skill (a wonderful yam pudding), the other a lesson in breast

weaning: their two-year-old son was raising hell because she had put hot pepper on her breast, and every time he tried to suck, he got a sting.

I noticed that C.K. was particularly moody tonight, and when I asked if anything was bothering him, he sullenly replied that he had asked the priest to christen his children with their African (Ewe) names (Salasie and Nunna) instead of the customary Johns, Josephs, and Marys, but was refused. "It just wasn't done." He had told the priest what he could do with his Christianity, but he was still brooding over it.

APRIL 28

Back from end-of the-month chores in town. I never realized before that Berekum had so many tailors. There must be at least a hundred scattered along the main streets, most of whom have only a kitchen table, some shears, a tape, and a hand-operated sewing machine.

Heard from a colleague that the Anglicized American posted in Sunyani got the boot. The Regional Commissioner had popped in unexpectedly on a staff meeting, and, learning that no Eastern countries were represented in their library, gave the guy his walking papers—despite protests from the staff that they had written to several Eastern embassies and got no reply.

This same colleague also tells me that our principal is in hot water with the party boys. He objected to their use of school chairs for their meetings: they were falling apart, he said—a remark that was construed to be definitely anti-party, having nothing at all to do with the issue of *chairs*. So, another one who's got to watch his step these days . . . I can't say my heart bleeds for the guy.

Just found out how Ghana's National Anthem was selected. The national committee appointed to choose among several songs that had been submitted was predominantly European (meaning not only whites, but also a large number of "European-oriented" Africans). Thus the Ghanaian had little choice in the matter, and though he raised a big stink when it was first sung in public, somehow it stuck. The African who had really pushed for it, I was told, was more "European than the Europeans." (And, if I know anything about human psychology, they probably despise him for it, too.)

Also got some new dope on the school administration. Seems that it was as corrupt as hell before the present principal took the reins out of the hands of the bursar's wife, who literally ran the place through her yes-man husband. They've had their hands in the till ever since the school opened (eleven years is more than enough time to learn how to fix the books), but, owing to the principal's vigilant eye, the school has saved 500 pounds in the past two months alone. By removing certain functions from his control, he's reduced the chap's income to a mere pittance—undoubtedly the reason for the bursar's resignation. But—get this—the principal has promised him a letter of recommendation. Too much!

I can't help thinking of the bursar in Half Assini. Maybe he was guilty of the charges brought against him after all . . . How else to explain a 20-pounds-per-month clerk's owning a large oil-palm plantation? Incidentally, the grapevine has it that he's resigned, too—to work on his farm! . . .

What a gas! The ed. teacher turns out to be the chief of

Sunyani in disguise. Certainly clears up a lot of things: why he is held in such high esteem by my colleagues, for one thing, why he is always regally dressed and carries himself with dignity at all times, and perhaps why I've received hostile looks from many of the staff when he and I were hashing out an argument. One just doesn't argue with a chief! Wonder why he never told me. If it hadn't been for his nephew, I probably never would have known. Nice kid . . . Told me all about his village. Seems that "Sunyani" means "place where elephants are hunted" in the Akan language; at one time, the boy said, this was big elephant country, and the powerful chief of Odumasi, a village a few miles away, governed both villages until quite recently, when the government gave Sunyani its own chief. A group of whites had once tried to settle in Odumasi, but a fetish priest who didn't like the idea worked a little *ju ju* on them. After a couple died, the rest fled to Sunyani, where they met a similar fate. And all the time I thought that mosquitoes were responsible for keeping would-be white settlers out of Ghana!

So ENDS MY DIARY—but not my stay—in Ghana. Another notebook, with entries for the months of May and early June, would be missing from my suitcase when I left for home. On the advice of a South African friend, who convinced me that certain people were out to hang me, I burned it along with some letters and news clippings. But there was one entry I'd be damned if I'd burn —Malcolm X's fiery speech to the students at the University of Ghana—for here was a fitting end to my stay, one that held the promise of a new beginning.

(From a tape of the speech of Malcolm X at the University of Ghana in May 1964, recorded by the French husband of one of the late Richard Wright's daughters.)

I intend for my talk to be very informal, because our position in America is an informal position [laughter], and I find that it is very difficult to use formal terms to describe a very informal position. No condition of any people on earth is more deplorable than the condition or plight of the twenty-two million black people in America. And our condition is so deplorable because we are in a country that professes to be a democracy and professes to be striving to give justice and freedom and equality to everyone who is born under its constitution. If we were born in South Africa or in Angola or some part of this

earth where they don't profess to be for freedom, that would be another thing; but when we are born in a country that stands up and represents itself as the leader of the Free World, and you still have to beg and crawl just to get a chance to drink a cup of coffee, then the condition is very deplorable indeed.

So tonight, so that you will understand me and why I speak as I do, it should probably be pointed out at the outset that I am not a politician. I don't know anything about politics, I'm from America but I'm not an American. I didn't go there of my own free choice [sustained applause]. If I were an American there would be no problem, there'd be no need for legislation or civil rights or anything else. So I just try to face the fact as it actually is and come to this meeting as one of the victims of America, one of the victims of Americanism, one of the victims of democracy, one of the victims of a very hypocritical system that is going all over this earth today representing itself as being qualified to tell other people how to run their country when they can't get the dirty things that are going on in their own country straightened out [sustained applause].

So if someone else from America comes to you to speak, they're probably speaking as Americans, and they speak as people who see America through the eyes of an American. And usually those types of persons refer to America, or that which exists in America, as the American Dream. But for the twenty million of us in America who are of African descent, it is not an American dream; it's an American nightmare [laughter].

I don't feel that I am a visitor in Ghana or in any part of Africa. I feel that I am at home. I've been away for four hundred years [laughter] but not of my own volition, not of my own will. Our people didn't go to America on the Queen Mary, we didn't go by Pan-American, and we didn't go to America on the Mayflower. We went in slave ships, we went in chains. We weren't immigrants to Amer-

ica, we were cargo for purposes of a system that was bent upon making a profit. So this is the category or level of which I speak. I may not speak it in the language many of you would use, but I think you will understand the meaning of my terms.

When I was in Ibadan [Nigeria], at the University of Ibadan last Friday night, the students there gave me a new name, which I go for—meaning I like it [laughter]. [Nigerian term] which they say means in Yoruba—if I am pronouncing that correctly, and if I am not pronouncing it correctly it's because I haven't had a chance to pronounce it for four hundred years [laughter]—which means in that dialect, "The child has returned." It was an honor for me to be referred to as a child who had sense enough to return to the land of his forefathers—to his fatherland and to his motherland. Not sent back here by the State Department [laughter] but come back here of my own free will [sustained applause].

I am happy and I imagine, since it is the policy that whenever a black man leaves America and travels in any part of Africa, or Asia, or Latin America and says things contrary to what the American propaganda machine turns out, usually he finds upon his return home that his passport is lifted. Well, if they had not wanted me to say the things I am saying they should never have given me a passport in the first place. The policy usually is the lifting of the passport. Now I am not here to condemn America, I am not here to make America look bad, but I am here to tell you the truth about the situation that black people in America find themselves confronted with. And if truth condemns America, then she stands condemned [hesitant but generous applause].

This is the most beautiful continent that I've ever seen; it's the richest continent I've ever seen, and strange as it may seem, I find many white Americans here smiling in the faces of our African brothers like they have been lov-

ing them all of the time [burst of laughter and scattered applause]. The fact is these same whites who in America spit in our faces, the same whites who in America club us brutally, the same whites who in America sic their dogs upon us, just because we want to be free human beings, the same whites who turn their water hoses upon our women and our babies because we want to integrate with them, are over here in Africa smiling in your face trying to integrate with *you* [muted laughter].

I had to write a letter back home yesterday and tell some of my friends that if American Negroes want integration, they should come to Africa, because more white people over here, white Americans, that is, look like they are for integration than there is in the entire American country [scattered laughter]. But actually what it is, they want to integrate with the wealth that they know is here—the untapped natural resources which exceed the wealth of any continent on this earth today. When I was coming from Lagos to Accra Sunday, I was riding on an airplane with a white man who represented some of the interests, you know, that are interested in Africa, and he admitted—at least it was his impression—that our people in Africa didn't know how to measure wealth, that they worship wealth in terms of gold and silver, not in terms of the natural resources that are in the earth, and that as long as the Americans or other imperialists or twentieth-century colonialists could continue to make the Africans measure wealth in terms of gold and silver, they never would have an opportunity to really measure the value of the wealth that is in the soil, and would continue to think that it is *they* who need the Western powers instead of thinking that is the Western powers who need the people and the continent that is known as Africa. The thing is, I hope I don't mess up anybody's politics or anybody's plots or plans or schemes, but then I think that it can be well proved and backed up.

Ghana is one of the most progressive nations on the African continent primarily because it has one of the most progressive leaders and most progressive presidents [loud applause]. The President of this nation has done something that no American, no white American, wants to see done—well, I should say "no American" because all the Americans over there are white Americans. President Nkrumah is doing something here that the government in America does not like to see done, and that is he's restoring the African image. He is making the African proud of the African image; and whenever the African becomes proud of the African image and this positive image is projected abroad, then the black man in America, who up to now has had nothing but a negative image of Africa—automatically the image that the black man in America has of his African brothers changes from negative to positive, and the image that the black man in America has of himself will also change from negative to positive. And the American racists know that they can rule the African in America, the African-American in America, only as long as we have a negative image of ourselves. So they keep us with a negative image of Africa. And they also know that the day that the image of Africa is changed from negative to positive, automatically the attitude of twenty-two million Africans in America will also change from negative to positive. And one of the most important efforts to change the image of the African is being made right here in Ghana. And the Ghanaian personality can be picked right out of any group of Africans anywhere on this planet, because you see nothing in him that reflects any kind of feeling of inferiority or anything of that sort. And as long as you have a President who teaches you that you can do anything that anybody else under the sun can do, you got a good man [loud but brief applause].

Not only that, we who live in America have learned

to measure black men: the object we use to measure him is the attitude of America toward him. When we find a black man who's always receiving the praise of the Americans, we become suspicious of him. When we find a black man who receives honors and all kinds of plaques and beautiful phrases and words from America, we immediately begin to suspect that person, because it has been our experience that the Americans don't praise any black man who is really working for the benefit of the black man, because they realize that when you begin to work in earnest to do things that are good for the people on the African continent, all the good you do for people on the African continent has got to be against someone else, because someone else up to now has benefited from the labor and the wealth of the people on this continent. So our yardstick in measuring these various leaders is to find out what the Americans think about them. And these leaders over here who are receiving the praise and pats on the back from the Americans, you can just flush the toilet and let them go right down the drain [laughter].

This President here is disliked. Don't think that it's just the American press, it's the government. In America when you find a concerted effort of the press to always speak in a bad way about an African leader, usually that press is actually reflecting government opinion. But America is a very shrewd government: if it knows that its own governmental position will cause a negative reaction from the people that it wants to continue to exploit, it will pretend to have a free press and at the same time sic that free press on a real African leader and stand on the sideline and say that this is not government policy. But everything that happens in America is government policy [burst of scattered laughter of disbelief].

Not only is the President of this country disliked, the President of Algeria, Ben Bella, is disliked because he is revolutionary, he's for freedom of everybody. Nasser is disliked because he's for freedom of everybody. All of them are referred to as dictators. As soon as they get the mass of their people behind them they're a dictator. As soon as they have unity of their people in their country they're a dictator. If there is no division, fighting, and squabbling going on, the leader of that country is a dictator if he is an African, but as long as it is in America, he's just an American President who has the support of the people [laughter and sustained applause].

I am coming to America in a minute, but I just want to comment on our relations I've noticed since being here. I heard that there is a conflict among some of our brothers and sisters over here concerning whether or not it's advisable for the government to play such a prominent role in guiding the education—the curriculum and what not—of the people of the country and in the various universities. Yes, anytime you have a people who have been colonized for as long as our people have been colonized, and you tell them now they can vote, they will spend all night arguing and never get anywhere. Everything needs to be controlled until the colonial mentality has been completely destroyed, and when that colonial mentality has been destroyed at least to the point where they know what they are voting for, then you give them a chance to vote on this and vote on that. But we have this trouble in America, as well as other areas where colonialism has existed, the only way they can practice or apply democratic practices is through advice and counsel.

So my own honest, humble opinion is, anytime you want to come out from under a colonial mentality, let the government set up the educational system and edu-

217

cate you in the direction or way they want you to go in, and then after your understanding is up to the level where it should be, you can stand around and argue or philosophize or something of that sort [laughter and applause].

There is probably no more enlightened leader on the African continent than President Nkrumah, because he lived in America. He knows what it is like there. He could not live in that land as long as he did and be disillusioned, or confused, or be deceived. Anytime you think that America is the land of the free, you come there and take off your national dress and be mistaken for an American Negro, and you will find out you're not in the land of the free [immediate and general applause]. America is a colonial power. She is just as much a colonial power in 1964 as France, Britain, Portugal, and all these other Europeans countries were in 1864. She's a twentieth-century colonial power; she's a modern colonial power, and she has colonized twenty-two million African-Americans. While there are only eleven million Africans colonized in South Africa, four or five million colonized in Angola, there are twenty-two million Africans colonized in America right now on May 13, 1964. What is second-class citizenship if nothing but twentieth-century colonialism? They don't want you to know that slavery still exists, so rather than call it slavery they call it second-class citizenship.

Either you are a citizen or you are not a citizen at all. If you are a citizen, you are free; if you are not a citizen, you are a slave. And the American government is afraid to admit that she never gave freedom to the black man in America and won't even admit that the black man in America is not free, is not a citizen, and doesn't have his rights. She skillfully camouflages it under these pretty terms of second-class citizenship. It's colonialism, neo-colonialism, imperialism . . . [spontaneous laughter].

One of our brothers just landed here today from New York. He told me that when he left New York, the police were walking in Harlem six abreast. Why? Because Harlem is about to explode. You know what I mean by "Harlem"? Harlem is the most famous city on this earth: there is no city on the African continent with as many Africans as Harlem. In Harlem they call it little Africa, and when you walk through Harlem, you're in Ibadan, everyone there looks just like you. And today the police were out in force, with their clubs. They don't have police dogs in Harlem, 'cause those kind of people who live in Harlem don't allow police dogs to come in Harlem [laughter]. That's the point, they don't allow police dogs to come in Harlem . . . They are troubled with the existence of little gangs who have been going around killing people, killing white people.

Well now, they project it abroad as an anti-white gang. No, it's not an anti-white gang, it's an *anti-oppression* gang. It's an *anti-frustration* gang. They don't know what else to do. They've been waiting for the government to solve their problems; they've been waiting for the President to solve their problems; they've been waiting for the Senate and the Congress and the Supreme Court to solve their problems; they've been waiting for Negro leaders to solve their problems; and all they hear are a lot of pretty words. So they become frustrated and don't know what to do. So they do the only thing they know how: they do the same thing the Americans did when they got frustrated with the British in 1776—liberty or death. This is what the Americans did; they didn't turn the other cheek to the British. No, they had an old man named Patrick Henry who said "liberty or death." I never heard them refer to him as an advocate of violence; they say he's one of the founding fathers, because he had sense to say "liberty or death," and there is a growing tendency among black Americans today, who

are able to see that they don't have freedom—they are reaching the point now where they are ready to tell the Man no matter what the odds are against them, no matter what the cost is, it's liberty or death. If this is the land of the free, then give us some freedom. If this is the land of justice, then give us some justice. And if this is the land of equality, give us some equality. This is the growing temper of the black American, of the African-American, of which there are twenty-two million.

Am I justified in talking like this? Let me see. I was in Cleveland, Ohio, just two months ago when this white clergyman was killed by the bulldozer. I was in Cleveland, I was there. Now you know if a white man in the garb, in the outfit, the custom, or whatever you want to call it, of a priest . . . if they run over him with a bulldozer, what will they do to a black man? They run over someone who *looks* like them who is demonstrating for freedom, what chance does a black man have? This wasn't in Mississippi, this was in Cleveland in the North. This is the type of experience the black man in America is faced with every day . . .

MY FIRST FEW MONTHS back in the States, I received the following letters, one from a village farmer who offered to "save" his seven-year-old daughter for me until I was ready for her, the other from the secretary at the school in Berekum.

14th. July, 1964

Dear Mr. Smith,

I have the most pleasure to indiet you this my few words. I will first of all thank you for all what you did to us during your stay in (GOVCO, Berekum) and I am sure we all shall remember you in words of prayer.

I will be glad also to tell you that, the person who you

took a photograph with, says his promise is still in his memory, that his *daughter* is still awaiting for you, until that you give a further authority to hand her to the other fellow.

I will endeavour to remember you and write you more letters if you reply to this my few lines.

I am sure to receive your letter, and try to enclose one letter for that man also.

I have the honour to be sir,
Yours sincerely,

21st December, 1964

Dear Mr. Smith

I will first render apology for my long silence, is all due to the delay of the Photographer who claimed to have short of postcards.

Dear Mr. Smith I have typed more of your address to the Senior Prefect who is now called Mr. S------- B-------, to distribute to the students, I think more will write to you after their holidays, they are closing down on the 18th. this December. He asked me whether I know something about their gift sent to you, it is a (Stool) well designed, from the Students.

Find the attached, the photo you requested, your Driver friend who donated his beloved daughter.

Dear Mr. Smith can you please buy me any kind of *Brain Pills* which you think is powerful for me, I am making preparation for Clerical Officers' Examination. It's English and Mathematics next year. I beg you to help me pass easily.

How is your life? Are you enjoying your studies in your university? Some people do ask where you are, they asked whether after studies you will come back to Ghana. I think you will remember a certain red coppered girl, (Yaa A---) she asked me where she can get your address at that time we were doubtful of your address. Am I to give her your address? And like I can next time send her photo to you.

Please accept my Christmas greetings, all of the Clerical Staff hail you and pray for your come back. I am sound and wish you the same.

Yours sincerely,